BEING HUMAN

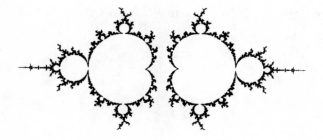

AN ENTHEOLOGICAL GUIDE TO GOD, EVOLUTION AND THE FRACTAL ENERGETIC NATURE OF REALITY

MARTIN W. BALL, PH.D.

Being Human: An Entheological Guide to God, Evolution, and the Fractal Energetic Nature of Reality

Martin W. Ball, Ph.D.

ISBN: 978-0-615-32803-4

Disclaimer:

This book is intended for educational and philosophical purposes. The author does not encourage, endorse, or support illegal or dangerous behavior of any kind and readers assume full responsibility for their choices and actions.

TABLE OF CONTENTS:

PART III, OPENING TO ENERGY WITH ENTHEOGENS

ENTHEOGENIC AFFIRMATIONS

INTRODUCTION

Congratulations!

You hold in your hands (or are perhaps reading on your computer screen) a genuine guide to fulfilling your nature as a human being. In writing this guide, my goal is to present to the reader a basic account of the true nature of reality without any fluff, fantasy, story, or unnecessary metaphysics or speculation, with the confidence that *this is the true knowledge that can liberate you from all illusion and the suffering illusion causes.* Much of what is written here is presented as matter-of-fact without much argumentation. It is my hope that readers will see the internal consistency and overall simplicity of what I am sharing and will find it easy to apply the principles and ideas presented herein to their lives, attain personal liberation, and find fulfillment and happiness.

However, it is not as simple as just reading this guide. Many of the ideas found herein will be challenging for you, especially if you are a practitioner of virtually any religion. Honestly, it might be easier for you if you are a scientific materialist atheist. Regardless, truly actualizing the wisdom presented in this guide in your own life will take dedication and a willingness to work through your illusions and your resistance to what is truly real.

Understanding reality is not about accepting certain ideas as true. It is not about intellect or belief. It is about experience, and understanding the contextual nature of experience. This guide will provide a clear map to how you can experience the ideas presented herein for yourself, in your own life, in each and every moment. It all begins with you and ends with you.

Are you ready to take responsibility for yourself and your life and enter into a true relationship with the fundamental nature of reality? If so, then this could be the guide for you. Set aside your beliefs, open your mind, take a deep breath, relax, and let's begin.

The Radical Non-Dualism of the Entheological Paradigm

As will become apparent throughout this guide, the view of reality being articulated here could best be described as "radical non-dualism." What this basically means is that "all things are one." While this is a common refrain of mystics and many spiritual practitioners, the actual implications of what this means has remained mystified. The difference between what mystics say and what is being presented here is that this guide will explain, without any mystification, precisely what it means that all things are one and how reality works as a coherent energetic system. A key to understanding this profoundly interconnected nature of reality is the energetic mathematics of fractals and geometry, as will be explained in much greater detail below (though no math or equations are presented in this guide). For now, it is enough to say that all of reality, everything we know scientifically and everything that we experience personally as life and consciousness, can be explained by the fundamental concept of fractal energy. In physics, this could be described as a "Grand Unified Theory," or GUT: A theory that is able to explain *everything*. However, this is even more powerful than any GUT developed *within physics,* for the physical sciences have no explanation for consciousness or life, whereas the Entheological Paradigm does and is therefore far more inclusive and comprehensive.

Another key concept is that this is an "entheological paradigm." Entheology is the "logic or study of God within." Paradigm means "exemplary model." Thus the model of reality being presented here is based on the concept that "God" is "within." This is a bit misleading, however, for in actuality, this model is not limiting the idea of God to being "within." In fact, God is not only within, but without as well. In reality, God is *all things*. It is thus the task of this guide to adequately explain how God, as energy, *is reality*. The implication, of course, is that *this includes you!*

So, we begin with you . . .

PART I

THE NATURE OF REALITY

<u>YOU</u>

Who Are You?

Who are you? And perhaps more importantly, *what* are you? You are certainly a human being, but what, exactly, is a human being? What does it mean to *be human?* What does it mean to *be you?*

There are many ways that one can answer these questions. One can look to religion, science, culture, tradition, psychology, spirituality, family, etc., and generate answers from these perspectives. These different perspectives provide very different answers, however, and many of them do not necessarily agree with each other, raising the question of the nature of truth. Science says that you are the product of random, purposeless evolution - ultimately an animal that somehow got smart. Religions might say that you are an incarnated soul on a divine mission to reach enlightenment or salvation. It is hard to see how these two perspectives could be reconciled.

In general, there is no real consensus in developing an answer to the questions above. It all seems to depend on perspective and there seems to be little room to bring disparate views into alignment with one another. Scientific, religious, and cultural views all seem to be in conflict with each other, all with their own assumptions, propositions, explanations, and expectations. There are many competing camps, and individuals usually choose where they feel they belong in the marketplace of ideas regarding the nature of being human with explanatory systems that reflect their concerns, values, and beliefs.

Is there no way to sort it out? Are the answers to these questions simply relative to one's perspective?

I am confident that there is a way to sort out these questions and that in the end, truth is far from relative. The purpose of this guide is to answer the question of "Who are you?" from a definitive perspective that is grounded in fundamental truth.

Who or What is God?

Though this may sound surprising at this point, the basic truth is that the answer to this question and the question of "Who are you?" is essentially the same.

Yes, that is correct.

YOU ARE GOD.

Startling, perhaps, but true.

However, this answer, at this point, doesn't really help, because it still requires that we answer the question of who, or what, God actually is. If one does not understand the true nature of God, then providing the answer that you are God does little to help in the way of personal understanding.

Therefore, in answering the question of "Who are you?" one must investigate the nature of God.

The Problem

If you are God, why is it that this is not your immediate experience? How can the "truth" be so seemingly different from our ordinary reality?

The simple answer is that this condition is a product of the ego. It is our egos that structure our reality into a fundamental illusion of separateness; that is their function. Due to our egos, we live in a basic state of paradox: simultaneously being both God and an individual "self" in a unique body. While this can be difficult for an ego to come to grips with and accept (as egos constantly seek self-validation to perpetuate the illusion of their existence), it is simply a basic truth of our existence and the sooner it is accepted, the sooner liberation, authenticity, and happiness will follow.

Though God is talked about in many religions, something that this guide will make clear is that the ideas of God as produced and circulated among religious traditions are largely the fantasy-based product of egos (and therefore not helpful when considering the true nature of the self, God, or reality). Religions have projected God "out there" as something "other" that must be obeyed, worshiped, and often feared. In short, most concepts of God are based on projections of the ego and have nothing at all to do with who and what this being actually is or what it is actually doing. This is especially true of the Western monotheistic traditions of Judaism, Christianity and Islam, which all have profoundly distorted notions of who or what God is.

The Incomplete Perspective of Science

The physical and empirical sciences are by far the most effective methods for understanding the physical nature of reality, far surpassing any other development in human cultures or history. Though all human cultures have had their own unique ways of conceptualizing and describing the world around them, no intellectual developments and methodologies have been as effective and fruitful as the scientific method of observation, theory building, testing, reviewing, and revising when it comes to producing collectively verifiable objective truth. While the specifics of scientific truth are always open to revision (with the introduction of new data or theories), the methodology is highly effective and can be pursued across cultures, regardless of one's beliefs, traditions, or spiritual and metaphysical views.

As a result, humans have garnered a great deal of verifiable, objective data about the physical world in which they live, and science has helped to reveal the physical mechanisms and properties at work in phenomena that were formally obscure or mystified through religious and cultural lenses. Things that were once understood to be the work of the spirits or acts of God are now easily understood as natural phenomena that function according to basic mathematical, chemical, or energetic laws.

Though overly simplified here, the basic scientific position is that ideas of entities like spirits, souls, gods and "God" are irrelevant for understanding the nature of reality. When the physical world is examined carefully, there appears to be no evidence for the existence of such entities. And following Occam's Razor, the maxim that the simplest explanation is usually the correct one and that theorists should not introduce unnecessary explanatory agents into their models, the conclusion is that spirits, souls and God are ultimately figments of the human imagination and are reflections of pre-scientific thinking.

The case might be closed if science could accurately explain how and why life developed, what consciousness is, where it comes from, why it exists, and why we are here at all to ponder these questions. However, upon even cursory examination, it is quite clear that science is fundamentally unable to answer these questions. The knowledge provided by science is therefore clearly limited.

This does not mean that science has nothing to say about the nature of life and consciousness, for it certainly does. Science can describe and map the evolutionary process. Science can describe the physical and chemical mechanisms at work in your brain and how your consciousness correlates with brain states. Psychologists can map out patterns in human thought and behavior. Biologists can tell us how different genes are related to different aspects of living beings.

However, these are all descriptions of physical mechanisms and processes. What we get from science regarding the actual nature of life and consciousness is not an explanation in any sense. Saying that biological life is a product of the natural laws of evolution explains nothing – it merely describes a process.

Consider the following question: If everything is made out of the same fundamental particles (as is claimed by quantum physicists), and there is NO FUNDAMENTAL DIFFERENCE between the particles that compose your body and the particles that make up a slab of cement (they're all quarks, electrons, protons, etc.), then how is it possible that you are alive and the cement isn't? Science has found no special "ingredient" that makes you alive, other than consciousness, and since consciousness is not a physical phenomenon, science has no way of studying or explaining it. At best, science can say that you are alive and the cement is not because you are a biological being with complex self-regulating systems. This, however, is merely a tautology and offers no explanatory power whatsoever.

Science, then, must be understood as providing absolutely no insight into why life or consciousness exists. At best, science can only describe the physical mechanisms through which the energies of consciousness and life appear to express themselves in biological beings. Life is still a fundamentally unanswered and unanswerable enigma in scientific theories of reality.

The Fantasy-laden Perspectives of Religions

Many people look to religion to provide them with the answers that cannot be forthcoming from the purely physical sciences. Religious traditions often purport to have exclusive access to "divine revelations" about the nature of life, its origins, and its destiny. Unlike science, however, which can be practiced by anyone regardless of beliefs, much of what religions have to offer depend on the adherence to basic "beliefs" and tenets of faith – things for which there is no evidence and no proof.

In generating their dogmas and worldviews, virtually all religions are at odds with each other to varying degrees. The basic truth is that the vast majority of what religions have to offer in terms of explanations for the nature of life and reality are based on inaccurate knowledge of the world we live in. Religions use myth, metaphor, symbol, allegory and other devices to communicate their particular view of the world and the responsibilities of being human. When taken as such, the perspectives offered by religions can be insightful. However, when they are taken literally, they become dogmatic expressions of faith that are beyond any rational argument, proof, or evidence.

Take, for example, the Biblical presentation of God creating the world in seven days. As a metaphor or symbol, that's fine, but if we are to take this literally, then we have to admit that there is absolutely no reason to believe that this is true other than the belief that the contents of the Bible were revealed by some divine being. Such an evidence-lacking belief would never be accepted by science, for obvious reasons. Unfortunately, from a modern, scientific perspective, the majority of what religions have to offer in terms of descriptions of reality fall into the same category of specious, evidence-lacking beliefs.

When it comes to describing what's "real," religions present us with fantastical realities. They speak of heavens, hells, spirit worlds, astral realms, spirits, souls, salvation, sin, reincarnation, resurrection, ascension, damnation, angels, guides, etc., etc. The difficulty is that while none of these ideas are observable from an objective standpoint, people do claim to have *experienced* such things, and therefore they must be real. But here we have a confabulation of experience with reality. Merely experiencing something is not equivalent to it being "real" in any objective sense. People are confused about what they experience all the time. And when religious claims are examined carefully, the claims of different religions clearly conflict and contradict each other.

When it comes to determining the nature of realty from a perspective we can all agree upon, religions do not seem to provide any real help – only mutually exclusive sets of propositions and beliefs that are, by their vary nature, unverifiable and tenets of faith. And what is worse, the vast majority of what religions describe as "reality" completely contradicts what is verifiably known through science.

If it weren't for the fact that religions make so many people miserable and that religious adherents are so often willing to kill each other over their fantasies, then religion could easily be dismissed as simply misguided human thinking. However, since religion does cause so many fundamental problems (despite whatever "good" it may provide to individuals, communities and cultures), helping religious believers to understand the truth of God is a necessary corrective for living harmoniously and happily in reality. For religious adherents to truly live in reality, much of what they claim will have to be understood for what it is: fantasy.

Resolution

A fundamental position of this guide to understanding the human experience is this: Physical sciences (particularly mathematical sciences) reveal basically true knowledge of the nature of reality, though there are limits to what this knowledge can be. Religions, on the other hand, while providing a few nuggets of truth and some good advice, are, for the most part, cultural constructions that reflect local and historical values, meanings, and concerns and have very little, if anything, to do with the actual nature of reality. In order for individuals to come to a clear understanding of the nature of reality, they have to understand both the limits of science and the illusions of religion.

It comes down to this: God is real (though no religion has accurately described who or what this being is), science is fundamentally true, but limited, and the majority of what religions have to offer (in terms of actual knowledge of the nature of reality) is pure ego-generated fantasy and speculation. Thus, to reach a resolution, the true nature of God (and thereby yourself) must be understood in order to come to genuine knowledge of the nature of reality.

To understand your true nature as God, you have to experience it. This guide will *describe* and *explain* the true nature of God and what it means for you, but in order to actually benefit from this knowledge, you must open yourself to the experience of being God, which is best described as being open to your true energy. The key to this process is personal work with entheogens, or substances that generate the experience of God within. With these tools, you can experience everything that will be shared in this guide directly for yourself with no religions, gurus, priests, or shamans standing between you and your direct experience of reality. The latter portion of this guide is dedicated to how you can navigate your way through this process and will also fully explore why entheogenic self-exploration is *the genuine path to personal awakening.* But before we get to the *how,* let's initially deal with the *what.*

Key Ideas

- Understanding yourself is the key to understanding everything
- You are God in embodied from
- Science cannot explain the existence of life or consciousness
- Religion is fantasy-laden and offers little for understanding the true nature of reality
- The method for coming to understand the true nature of reality is through direct experience and self-exploration
- Entheogens provide unparalleled tools for self-exploration

GOD AND EVOLUTION

God

In order to begin, set aside any previous ideas of who or what you think God is. Traditional religious views on God are largely not much help in understanding who or what God is as they are mostly ego projections that have been separated from the self, depicting God as something *mysteriously and enigmatically Other*. Nothing could actually be further from the truth. The reality of God is the most intimate thing in existence – indeed, *all of reality is God, including you and the moment you are experiencing right now*. There is absolutely nothing *other* about this. God, simply put, is *what actually is*. God *is reality*.

But let's get more specific. Saying that God is everything isn't necessarily helpful as it is such a general comment. So let's begin by describing God.

First and foremost, God is a *being*. God is not an abstract principle, a philosophical necessity, or a featureless, contentless consciousness that is fundamentally empty. God is a *being*. This means that God is self-aware and possesses will and intention and is able to actualize itself and its goals. And not only is God *a being*, but it is, in truth, *the being*. God is the *only being that actually exists*. All other beings are expressions and embodiments of this *one being*.

This *one being* is perfectly self-aware. God knows full well that *it* is the *only* being that exists and that *all things* are *it*. Because of this, there is no fear or judgment in God in any way whatsoever. God has nothing but love for itself. God actually is love, or perhaps more accurately, self-love. There is nothing that is not God and God loves all aspects of itself.

Second, God is energy. Everything that exists is a form of energy. There are many different kinds of energy and many different spectrums of energy, but in one way or another, everything that exists can be described as energy. We know from physics that all things we perceive as mass or as solid objects are actually just stable patterns of energy. Life, also, is energy, as are thoughts, feelings, sensations, expressions, actions, and consciousness itself. All things are energy. The *source* for all forms of energy is God, and God is energy (somewhat paradoxically).

Third, God is what we might call "the multi-being." God is one, but God has the ability to take multiple forms simultaneously, and thus is the "multi-being." The energy of life and consciousness that animates every living being in existence has its source in God, and actually is God in embodied form. Religions teach us that we have souls or spirits that give us life. This is fundamentally incorrect. Your life *is God*. You do not have a spirit or a soul in any way whatsoever. You are God in a body. Any idea of a soul or spirit is superfluous, unnecessary, and ultimately incorrect. Every living being is God embodied directly from source

Another way of saying this, which will be explored in greater detail shortly, is that *God is evolution itself.* Anyone who believes that there is some kind of conflict between God and evolution simply has no idea what they are actually talking about and could not be more fundamentally misguided by ego-projected fantasy of who and what God is or how God works. God has been evolving its form as a physical being for several billion years and has reached its current apex in us, in humanity. There is no conflict of any kind between God and evolution and any such notion is absurd.

Fourth, God is geometry and mathematics and is perhaps best described as a fractal energy being. Basic mathematical structures are the ontological foundation of reality. As such, mathematics, geometry and fractals were not *invented* by humans but rather *discovered*. All energy functions according to mathematical principles. This is why we are able to have sciences such as physics. Mathematical permutations of energy are simply how reality works. The more one understands how energy and mathematics work, especially fractals, the more one understands how the energy being of God truly functions to create and sustain physical and experiential reality.

Fifth, God is *NOW*. Neither the past nor the future exists. God is the ever-unfolding moment of *now*, which is precisely where all permutations of energy exist. Energy, by its nature, is never static. It is always changing in relation to what immediately preceded it in the flow of now. As such, there is nothing that is permanent. All energy is constantly changing and fluctuating. The only thing that persists is the ever-changing energy of now.

Sixth, God is pure self-actualization. God is doing one thing and one thing only: being itself in every way it can. In other words, all of reality happens when God is simply being itself. God has no other purpose or goal. Everything that God does is just being itself. In this sense, we could describe all of reality as the life of God being itself. Reality and everything we experience is God doing its thing to be itself as it is expressed right now in the current moment. Nothing more, nothing less. Absolute, total and complete self-expression and actualization. There is nothing for God to do other than be itself.

And since YOU ARE GOD, that also means that there is nothing for you to do other than be yourself. But learning how to do that is both a simple and monumental task. How to realize this goal of being yourself will be the focus of the latter portions of this guide. First, we need to understand the way that God functions in reality before we can properly address how to successfully be you.

Key Ideas

- God is a being, not an abstract concept
- God is energy
- God is self-aware
- God is evolution
- God is mathematics
- God is the epitome of self-actualization

Radial Geometry and Inorganic Evolution

Let's talk about how reality works. For this, we can turn to both science and to the description of God given above to provide a reasonably accurate picture of how we went from nothing to the very moment of right now. So, let's start before the beginning . . .

Given that time is a function of manifest reality (or the world in which we live), we can't really talk about the "time" before the beginning. So, the "before" shouldn't necessarily be taken literally, but what I want to call to mind is that indeterminate state of being that existed "before" the universe we live in came to be.

For whatever reason, perhaps some kind of paradoxical, self-referential choice, God realized that it existed, and not only that, that it was the *only thing* that existed. "I Am!" proclaimed this being to itself, and it was. But since this being was the only thing that existed, there was only one thing for it to do, and that was be itself. There was nowhere to go, nothing to do, and certainly no one to talk to or share the unique experience of being with. And since God knew that it was the only thing in existence, it knew that it had nothing to fear from being itself, so it chose to be itself fully, completely, and perfectly.

And that's when everything started. From the singularity that is God came a tremendous outpouring of pure energy, moving out in radial rays of mathematical permutations, constantly flowing and changing. As this energy expanded, space and time came into existence and the energy rapidly started changing form, cooling off, and collecting into new patterns of energy that had not previously existed in actuality, but only in potential form. It was this grand act of self-expression that moved reality from the potential state that existed within the being of God to the actual state of the universe and reality in which we find ourselves today. It was the beginning of fractal permutations of energy, forming itself into coherent patterns.

As the energy cooled off and became more stable, it started to form into the most basic of geometric shapes: the sphere. The sphere is the most basic as the limits of the energetic structure are all equidistant from the center, or the singularity that is God. Thus, as the energy of the early universe was cooling off and stabilizing, spheres and variations on spheres and spherical energetic structures became the basic building blocks of reality as energy moved from the state of possibility and potential into the state of actuality. Today, we would call these basic energetic structures quarks, sub-atomic particles, electrons, protons, etc., all repetitions of patterns in the fundamental fractal geometry.

These then started to coalesce into more and more stable structures with more complex energetic arrangements, and from these energetic processes, we got the chemical elements as listed on the periodic table of elements, the basic building blocks of physical reality. These then were able to interact and conglomerate into larger and larger structures, eventually giving rise to the large-scale structures of the universe such as stars, planets, etc.

All through this process, God, as energy, is simply being itself. Energy can only be true to itself. Energy can't be something other than what it is. For example, if you have 12 volts of electricity, you have 12 volts of electricity. It will never be anything else. It can only be exactly what it is.

The way that energy works in the process of being itself is what we call, from our human perspective, natural laws, or the laws of physics or of mathematics. This is simply the given nature of reality as an energetic construct. It's just the way things work. God is energy. Energy is mathematical. Reality is energy. Reality is mathematical. God is mathematical.

Perhaps the most important mathematical function to understand is that of fractals. Fractals are complex mathematical formulas that map out repetitions and variations on patterns across multiple scales simultaneously. Mathematicians were quite astounded when, with the development of fractal mathematics, suddenly, here was a construct that allowed for the mathematical mapping of what were previously assumed to be somewhat chaotic and random systems. Clouds, for example, can be mathematically mapped with fractals. So can coast lines, mountain ranges, river systems, and possibly even the energetic foundations of quantum physics. In other words, when the basic geometric forms of spheres start to interact energetically, they naturally form fractal formations: repetitions and variations of patterns across multiple scales simultaneously. Energy, when simply being itself and following "natural laws," forms fractals.

There is one more interesting and significant geometric feature of the non-biological universe, and that is crystals. Crystals are unique in the non-living energetic environment for not only do they exhibit complex geometry, but they also *grow*. Physically, crystals are natural amplifiers, transmitters, and conduits of energy. Crystals are able to process energy in ways that other forms of physical matter are not. They are decidedly unique and significant and their complex geometry is integral in their ability to move energy.

The Geometry of Early Organic Evolution

The energetic evolution of the inorganic structures of the universe took many billions of years worth of energetic transformation. In other words, God, as an energy being, could not create the universe fully formed as we now experience it. God, as energy, had to work according to basic energetic, geometric and mathematical laws. This is because *God is energy* and is not able to be anything other than itself. The mythical notion of a "creator God" who snapped "his" "fingers" and suddenly the universe appeared fully formed is precisely that – a myth and a story. It has nothing to do with how God actually works according to its true nature. God cannot be anything other than what it is, and it is not some distant being that just made the universe, "poof." God is the energy that is continually transforming itself through the ever-flowing moment of now.

With the eventual formation of the stable energetic structures that we can now identify as comprising our universe, God reached an interesting point in the transformation of energy. Metaphorically speaking, God had succeeded in making a fantastic mansion out of itself and its energy, but other than the energy transferred and amplified by crystal formation, God had no actual "perspective" within the mansion. To put it crudely, God built this fantastic mansion out of itself, but still had the pressing question of "how do I get in to enjoy this universe?"

That is precisely what biological evolution is for: it is the energetic mechanism that God is using to get *inside* itself as distinct, living beings, in order for God to play the reality game as multiple "characters" simultaneously (much like when we dream, we are all the characters in our dreams, as well as the total environment and context of the dream, though we usually only personally identify with one specific perspective that we identify as our "self" through the imposition of our ego).

How did God do it? The answer is quite simple: God used crystals.

The universe is a great big place, and while it may be statistically probable that there is life on other planets, the *only* planet that we *actually know of* that harbors life is our beautiful home, Planet Earth. Therefore, an account of reality as we know it does not need to account for life anywhere else. It is important to make clear then that all descriptions of the evolution of life need only address what we know of here on this planet. We only need account for the actual evidence.

Using crystals as a sort of inorganic sensory organ, God felt around for the best place to begin the next phase of the reality game. What God needed was the right environment where the vibrations of the energy of consciousness could best be accommodated in the physical universe. It wasn't that God was looking to introduce consciousness, for rudimentary levels of consciousness exists in energy by its very nature, but in order for consciousness to process large amounts of self-referential data within the physical system, it needs a complex energetic structure to filter energy and information through. In other words, it needs more complex formations than those provided by inorganic matter in order for it to be expressed fully in physical reality.

The environment with all the necessary conditions was found right here on Earth. The planet was the proper distance from its nearby star, for one, but more importantly, the majority of its surface was covered in a liquid crystalline matrix that was ideal for processing the energy of life and consciousness. Saltwater is a combination of two crystalline forms: salt and water. A perfect energetic environment, when mixed with the right amount of sunlight.

It was here, in our oceans, that God began to evolve itself as living beings. As with the inorganic universe, God started with simple, radial geometry. Single-celled organisms, or basic spheres, were the first to arrive on the scene. Another complex crystalline structure developed inside these early spheres. This structure would encode information and map out future permutations of these living energetic being and functions as a holographic encoder: DNA.

Thus began biological evolution. Working with spheres in the ideal energetic crystalline environment, God made a great deal of headway in the evolutionary process. Single-celled organisms began interacting and forming symbiotic relationships, eventually recombining into multi-celled organisms. This allowed for more complex geometric formations of living beings, and once organisms moved past the single-celled stage, they started to develop, just as with the inorganic universe, into fractal forms. Life eventually moved out of the oceans, but brought the ocean with it in the saltwater that composes the bulk of living bodies.

All living beings, just like structures in inorganic nature, are fractal/geometric forms. Early life is based on radial, spiral, and branch forms of geometry that grow according to fractal patterns, such as plants, sea creatures, coral, etc. The basic geometry of early life is fractal forms that are embodiments of God's nature as an energetic being.

The evolutionary potential of early life was limited, however. The energetic structures produced by radial, spiral, and branch fractal geometry were not sophisticated enough to process complex energetic relations as required by high levels of conscious awareness. Thus, for the most part, early life forms, and especially plants, are best understood as living energy transformers. Early life was busy transforming energy in ways to make the necessary energetic foundation for more complex forms of life. It was laying the groundwork for the radical potential of evolution.

The Geometry of Higher Evolutionary Forms

Eventually, conditions were energetically right for the next stage: the introduction of infinity loops as an energetic organizing structure.

The infinity loop is a stunning variation on the sphere. Imagine taking a sphere and pinching and twisting it. This is how you get an infinity loop. Now, instead of energy radiating from the center out in all directions simultaneously, the energy moves through the center, out one loop, crosses back through the center, and then goes out through the other loop, and then back again, endlessly circulating and always referencing back to the center, the source. It becomes an infinite loop of energy and actually looks like our symbol for infinity, "∞."

The infinity loop became the energetic model for all higher life forms and is what allowed for the development of both bilateral symmetry and a centralized nervous system. Without infinity loops, the ability of physical beings to process the infinite possibilities of the energy of God as a conscious, self-aware being would not have been physically possible.

The geometry is like this: take a spiral and unwind it. Now you have a line. On that line, stack your infinity loops, with the center of the infinity loop resting on the unwound spiral line. You now have the basic energetic model of higher life forms with bilateral symmetry.

The unwound spiral eventually evolved into the spinal column of the central nervous system, and the infinity loops evolved into our basic physical features of two hemispheres of the brain, two eyes, two ears, two nostrils, the chambers of the heart, the lungs, the sexual organs, and our basic anatomy of shoulders, elbows, wrists, hands, hips, knees, ankles and feet. Infinity loops were clearly a major upgrade in the energetic blueprint of living beings. Beings were able to process far more information, they became more mobile, they developed more conscious awareness of their physical world through their sense organs (as based on infinity loops), and therefore became much more suitable vehicles for God to get around in as they more accurately reflected God's nature as a self-aware, conscious, living being that can exercise free will in its process of being itself.

And God had a *great* time. Dinosaurs were a lot of fun. They could swim, fly, run, crawl, climb, etc. There was a lot for God to do in those forms and evolution progressed nicely.

The only problem was those big lizards weren't very smart. After millions of years, their potential as true God vehicles just wasn't quite satisfying.

So, this is when God introduced dimethyltryptamine into the mix.

Mammalian Evolution and Dimethyltryptamine

Dimethyltryptamine, or DMT, as it is commonly called, is listed as a Schedule I illegal drug in the United States and is prohibited in most other countries around the world as well. When consumed, it becomes a powerful mind-altering agent and is therefore considered a "drug" by the powers that be. The irony is that DMT is perhaps one of the most important developments in all of evolution, and, without it, there would not be a single human being on this planet today. In many respects, humans, as well as all other mammals, are DMT beings.

In the grand scope of evolution, mammals had some new features. They were covered with hair. They gave birth to live young and nursed them. They were warm blooded. And, not insignificantly, all mammals have DMT and 5-MeO-DMT (5-methoxy-dimethyltryptamine) in their blood, lungs, spinal fluid, brains, and on their nerves throughout their nervous system. The presence of DMT in mammals was a major evolutionary step.

DMT and 5-MeO-DMT are, in their physical form, crystals. They are also tryptamines, or neurotransmitters. In other words, they are crystals that process the energy of consciousness and awareness. It is not an accident that forms of DMT are in our nervous system. It is what allows us to process the energy of the conscious experience of being in our bodies. It is also what allows us to experience higher forms of consciousness and perception. In many respects, we could characterize our experience of ordinary reality as being a low-level DMT trip! When you add more DMT or 5-MeO-DMT to the system, either through ingestion of a substance or through various techniques of achieving endogenous (in-the-body) releases of DMT, our perception of energy and our conscious experience changes radically. Much more will be said about this in the latter portions of this guide.

With the introduction of mammals onto the evolutionary scene, God now had a whole new set of possibilities to work with. These mammals had true potential to develop as conscious and self-aware beings. In other words, they had far more potential to be true God vehicles than other previous evolutionary developments. Dinosaurs were around for millions of years and didn't get much smarter. Mammals, however, were ready to take off and begin something truly special.

Human Evolution and the Ego

Eventually, some of those mammals started to get really, really smart. They were becoming more and more aware of their environment, and through evolution, developed these things we call hands, which really opened up a new realm of possibilities. Animals were no longer limited to crude manipulations of the physical world with simple appendages or with their mouths, but now they could truly start to change the environment, according to their will, with their hands. These mammals started to walk upright, and make things with their hands. The potential was enormous. And they were getting smarter.

Now it was time for the next big development. These creatures who were getting pretty smart held a lot of potential as God vehicles. However, to truly be a self-responsible God vehicle (a being truly "created in the image of God" as a responsible, self-aware energy being), they had to understand themselves as existing as individual beings. They had to be self-aware.

Thus came the ego. It is important to point out right away that the ego is not the personality. Personality generates from your genes and what you inherit from your parents and ancestors. All mammals, in general, have some capacity to express personality. The smarter the animal, the more the personality, or unique behavioral characteristics, shows and is able to express itself. But the personality is not the ego, so even though higher mammals have personalities, they do not have egos and are therefore largely unable to reflect on themselves as unique beings. In other words, they don't ever think about how they are expressing their personalities. They are merely expressing themselves, and in so doing, are perfectly being themselves. It is humans, with our egos, who reflect on our behavior and experience and understand that it is "I" who is experiencing and expressing these things.

The ego, then, is a self-referential and self-validating energetic construct within consciousness. It is also fundamentally an illusion, though it is an evolutionarily necessary one in the development of human consciousness. The ego functions by creating separations between what it chooses to identify as "me" and "not me." It generally becomes very protective of that which it identifies as "me" and is wary and cautious of what is "not me," for anything that is "not me" has the potential to harm or destroy "me." The ego also constantly seeks to validate its distinctions in any way that it can, and when its validations are threatened, it reacts with fear and energetic contraction to maintain the integrity of the illusion of the separate self.

Without the ego, humans would never have been able to stand up and say, "I am!" However, that realization then led to a number of questions, such as, where did I come from? Where am I going? What is this crazy universe I find myself in?"

In other words, the ego is the starting point for God to wake up to itself in the dream, but it is also the mechanism that does everything it can to keep individual beings from realizing their true nature, because its very function is to create illusion. Anything that threatens that illusion can be profoundly disturbing for egos. This is why the fantasies spun by religions are far easier for egos to accept than the basic truth that they are embodiments of God and must be responsible for themselves. It is sooooo much more comforting for an ego to hear that some great being that exists outside itself and will reward it for good behavior or grant it favors if it prays or worships hard enough for, ultimately, everything is in this superior being's hands. Religions, like alcohol, are profoundly intoxicating for egos and affirm their illusions grandly. Any individual who truly wants to understand the actual nature of reality *must transcend the ego*. It is also the path to genuine liberation and happiness.

Ego Formation in Children

Though this is a topic that deserves far more attention than it will be given here, let us touch on the topic of children.

When children come into the world, they naturally want to do only a limited number of things: sleep, eat, and play. As with other mammals and higher animals, they come into the world with the possibilities of their personality already encoded in their genes. They start to learn how to express their personality by observing the behaviors of others, and their eager minds start to create strategies for how to engage others and the world that surrounds them. It is through this process that their egos eventually come into being.

However, children, with their superb powers of observation, quickly learn that, essentially, no one is honestly expressing how they really feel. They observe people saying one thing, but clearly feeling and thinking another. They realize that people rarely express themselves honestly, and when they finally do, it often comes out in forms that are explosive, angry, judgmental, and overly emotional. Their minds struggle to make sense of this peculiar situation. They learn very quickly that *everyone seems to be playing some kind of game where they willingly engage in manipulation, repression, sublimation, and lack of personal authenticity and responsibility*. In other words, they learn that people are trapped in playing ego games. If they want to fit in, which of course they do, they understand that they too must play the game. Before parents even realize it, their children start to manipulate them using sophisticated ego games.

What we have here is a fundamentally vicious cycle. Parents with confused egos raise children with confused egos and the cycle of illusion, manipulation, and suffering goes round and round. Therefore, if parents really want to take responsibility for raising healthy children, then they need to take responsibility for themselves and for the patterns of their egos. The best thing a parent can do for a child is to be a healthy and responsible role model. But they can't do that if they haven't taken the time to become responsible for themselves. All responsibility begins with self-responsibility.

God's Signature in Fractal Anatomy

Let us return for a moment to our characterization of God. God is a being of infinite energy that functions according to mathematical/fractal/geometric expressions. To put it very simply, from the infinite come fractal patterns. This is the basic nature of God and the basic nature of reality.

Coincidentally (or "only naturally"), a clear representation of this concept is in our very anatomy.

Let's take a closer look at the human body and how the energy of God works in human form. Consider first God's infinite mind. The capacity of God's consciousness is infinite, but even so, the energy of consciousness still works according to fractal/mathematical patterns. All things might be possible in the mind of God, but energy still works in particular ways.

This "signature" of the true nature of God is present anatomically in our very bodies. Understanding that your personal consciousness and awareness is God means accepting that your consciousness and awareness originates directly from source, with no intermediary functions. So, if we ask, "Where does the energy of consciousness in your brain come from?" the answer is, "God, the infinite source of all energy." Consciousness clearly does *not* come from the food you eat, the parts that make up your body, or anything else. Consciousness is not an "ingredient" in the physical world. It comes directly from source, from God.

Human anatomy literally shows us this "signature." Consciousness, while mediated through the entire body, is localized energetically in our brains as the central processing center. As stated before, the anatomical structure of the brain is an infinity loop placed on top of an unwound spiral (the spinal column). As the seat of our consciousness, the brain physically embodies the symbol of infinity. Then, branching out from the brain and the spinal column in a fractal branch pattern is the nervous system. This is God's signature. From the infinite, come fractal patterns of energy and manifestation.

We find the same signature in the cardio-vascular system. God is the infinite source of love and life. With the heart, we have two infinity loops stacked on top of each other with the upper and lower chambers of the heart. We also have the lungs, which are also infinity loops (which supply oxygen, or necessary energy, to the blood). These sets of infinity loops then branch out in the fractal branch pattern of our vascular system. Once again, we find the same signature: from the infinite source of energy come fractal patterns of energy and manifestation.

The third place we can find God's signature is in the sexual organs. For the male, we have the infinity loops of the testes and the two sides of the penis. For the female, we have the "lips" of the vagina and the ovaries. Here the infinite energy of evolutionary development is embodied in the infinity loops of our sexual anatomy. But where is the fractal pattern of energy that is God's method of manifesting energy in physical reality? The fractal pattern of energy that extends from the sexual organs is evolution itself, as well as the total physical body. Your physical body, which is organized according to the geometric principles of the golden ratio, is a fractal manifestation of energy from your parents' sexual organs. And when taken collectively, all of life and the grand sweep of evolution is the fractal pattern of energy that sexual reproduction gives rise to.

What is God Doing?

God has clearly been building better and better vehicles (living beings) through the ongoing process of evolution. In humans, evolution has reached a transcendent state. We have the capacity to self reflect on the nature of our existence. And because of that, we also have the capacity to transcend the limitations of the illusion and realize our true natures as embodiments of God. We are the epitome of the ultimate God vehicle at this point in evolution.

It seems reasonable to conclude that *this is precisely what God has been working for* in terms of evolution. God has been evolving all of reality and living beings in order for God to be fully actualized in physical form. This has been achieved in the human vehicle. Evolution is now ready for the next step: vehicles that can take responsibility for who and what they truly are. We are ready to more truly be ourselves as embodiments of God.

In terms of taking responsibility, humans are certainly in their infancy. Through our religions and myths, we have been telling ourselves fairytales about our existence and our responsibilities. These myths and fairytales have served to organize cultures and provided guidelines for thinking and acting to humans in ways that have been both fruitful and creative, as well as destructive and repressive. However, just like with a human child, eventually, you have to tell them that Santa Claus isn't real and it is time to take a more adult perspective on life.

The same is fundamentally true for humanity. It is time for us to move out of the illusions and fantasy and into reality so that we can truly take responsibility for ourselves. It is time to grow up.

If we can step up to the challenge and take responsibility, then the potential for evolution into ever-more conscious forms of God in a body becomes a true possibility. Consider that in truth, we are the one energy being that is everything. In theory, the more responsibility we can take for ourselves and the more control we can have over our own energy, the more we will be able to do in this energetic reality game that we are all busy playing. In other words, awakening to the true nature of reality may just be the beginning of where we might go from here. The possibilities are endless.

Consider also that we know of only one planet in the entire universe that harbors life. Though statistically it seems unlikely, what if this is the only planet with life on it? What if this is God's cosmic nest egg? Is it possible that God is planning on using our evolution as conscious beings to begin the process of populating the rest of the cosmos? If so, we will need clear minds and good science to accomplish this grand task, and we will need to take responsibility for who and what we are.

Ultimately, such speculation is largely irrelevant, though it is interesting. Our main concern is to get clear, here and now. The future will be what the future will be, and in any case, it is quite clear that God is doing *something* with evolution, and whatever that something is, it certainly serves God's purpose of fully being itself. It is important to understand that in the end, that is all God is doing: being itself. That is also all that we ever need do as embodiments and vehicles for God.

Key Ideas

- All of evolution, inorganic and organic, is an on-going process of energetic transformations and interactions that function according to basic mathematical and geometrical laws
- Fractal mathematics and geometry is the underlying mathematical foundation of all aspects of reality
- All living beings are embodiments of God
- There is only one source of all life and consciousness: God
- Higher life forms with centralized nervous systems are built on the bilateral symmetry of infinity loops and fractal branches
- Egos are necessary for conscious self-awareness
- Egos function to create the illusion of separation
- Egos provide individuals with a unique perspective
- Egos can be transcended
- Egos and personalities are distinct

PART II

LIVING IN REALITY

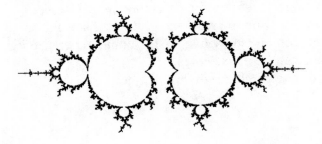

LIFE AS AN INDIVIDUAL

Understanding Your Vehicle

God, as the multi-being, has many different vehicles for it to experience the reality of itself in. Every unique individual living being is a vehicle that is powered directly from source, from God. Aside from humans, all other vehicles are just being themselves within their evolutionary and biological parameters. A tree is just busy being a tree and a cat is just busy being a cat. Neither has to think about what it means to be a cat or a tree. They are just fully themselves. They are perfect vehicles, in their limited capacity way. Human vehicles, because they have egos and are self-aware, have a great deal more choice about how they express themselves and manage their vehicles. They also have a great deal more potential for confusing themselves and making themselves unhappy. While there certainly are "natural disasters" that humans are subject to as embodiments of God playing the reality game, the vast majority of problems that humans encounter are purely self-generated. We are our own worst enemy.

A starting point for understanding how to avoid creating problems for ourselves as vehicles for God to experience reality in is to understand how our vehicle functions. If there is something wrong with your car or it is having problems, you take it to a mechanic to see if it is functioning properly. Similarly, given that human beings are God vehicles, understanding the mechanics of God's energy can help to resolve problems that individual vehicles may be experiencing.

Addressing the energy of your vehicle is a far more effective route than going on a retreat, doing a workshop, joining a religion, or seeing a therapist. When your car is having trouble, you take it to a mechanic, not a guru or a priest. Your body is a vehicle too, so why not treat it accordingly?

As a vehicle for God to walk around in and enjoy reality with, your body has three "divine" energy centers. These are the energy centers that anatomically shape into infinity loops. Thus, we have consciousness (the brain), life and love (heart and lungs) and creation/evolution (sexual organs). These are the three centers where the infinite energy of God directly interfaces with our bodies. These centers belong to God, so to speak, and the best that we can do is manage the energy present there. We cannot personally control it (you can't stop yourself from thinking, or stop yourself from breathing or your heart beating, or keep yourself from feeling sexual energy). At best, we can influence how this energy is allowed to flow through us, but we cannot ever stop these energies as long as we are in physical bodies. And given that we only experience anything by being in a physical body, these infinite sources of energy are our constant companions and are what give us life, awareness and consciousness.

As a physical being, we have two other primary energy centers, but these are not energy centers that are directly related to source and are more closely related with our individual vehicles. These are your "personal" energy centers and they function very differently from the three listed above. The first of these is the mouth and throat. Geometrically, this is a tube, not an infinity loop. In many respects, physical bodies are reality processors, or tubes. From the tube, they put things into reality and take other things out. Your mouth, energetically, is an input/output mechanism. With your mouth, you both literally consume physical reality as food and energetically, we "consume" aspects of reality that we are attracted to. Both literally and metaphorically, the mouth embodies what we "take in."

As an output mechanism, the mouth is our primary means of intentional energetic expression through vocalization and language. Much of what we do with our hands becomes an extension of the mouth. We use our hands to put things into our mouths and also use our hands to create art, music, writing, etc., as extensions of our innate expressive ability and communicative function as conscious beings.

It is the mouth/throat energy center that is the biggest problem for humans as this center affects everything else. This is your most personal energy center, for this is where you are determining what to take in and what to put out. It regulates your self-expression and thereby influences all the other energies of your system. From a purely physical standpoint, this is very easy to accept as true. What you put in your mouth will profoundly affect all the rest of the energy in your body. If you eat healthy food, your physical system is nourished and your energy functions better. If you drink poison, your physical system will shut down and you die, thereby short-circuiting the divine energy centers that are providing you with life.

The situation is more complicated when it comes to the output function because it is primarily here that the ego gets in the way. For example, let's say that your personality energetically resonates with the act of singing. You *love to sing* and want to sing as much as possible. You *want* to feel that energy vibrating through your body and filling the space around you. However, your roommate has been quite blunt with you: "You suck! You can't sing!"

How does ego react? There are a variety of ways. One is to shut down. You feel bad, so you stop singing, and then you feel sorry for yourself. Another option is to compromise and agree not to sing when your roommate is around (even if you really feel the urge), though this will probably make you feel unsatisfied and inauthentic. Yet another response is to sing more often with the intent of showing your roommate that you are not intimidated by their critique, which will probably aggravate a passive aggressive situation and drama will ensue.

If you have transcended your ego, then this situation will be no problem whatsoever. You will tell your roommate that you are fulfilling your desire to be authentic with yourself and your energy. You are taking responsibility for the energy inside you and expressing it in a healthy way. If you can't sing, that is your roommate's problem, but not yours, for you are satisfied and confident in your self expression, regardless of how it actually sounds.

Most people, in most situations, when confronted with an ego challenge, do not respond from a position of ego transcendence. People are so locked into the illusions and fantasies created by their egos that drama almost always ensues (if not immediately, then somewhere down the road). It is *only* the ego that creates such dramas. If a dog wants to bark, it will. It won't stop to think about whether it's the thing it should or shouldn't do. Shoulds and shouldn'ts are primarily ego concerns, especially when it comes to personal behavior or choice.

The last energy center is your stomach. This is a continuation of the tube of your mouth/throat center. What goes in and out of the mouth affects the stomach, or your physical processing center. When you eat rotten food, your stomach hurts. When you say ugly and hurtful things, you get stomach cramps and digestive discomfort. The ways you choose to use your input/output energy center will *always* affect your physical experience in your body, in one way or another.

So, your vehicle has three divine energy centers that are the sources of your energy, life, and conscious experience. These are organized into your central core and process electromagnetic energy (sexual attraction, brain waves and heart beat/pulse). We can influence these centers, but ultimately we cannot completely control them. And they are all physical expressions of infinite energy. Given that we, as humans, are the epitome of God in embodied form, we are also able to reach back into infinity through these energy centers. We can experience infinite consciousness, infinite love, and infinite sexual ecstasy. Through these centers, we can become full expressions of God in physical form.

With the other two centers, also aligned along our central core, we have the regulation of our personal expression and our physical being. These centers don't radiate energy as the divine centers do. Rather, they process and transform energy and translate it from one form to another: food turns into nourishment, our words express our thoughts and feelings, etc.

The arms and legs then become extensions of these energy centers and are primarily energy conduits for the energy that moves from our central core. With our hands, we are able to engage our environment at a physical/energetic level. Through our feet, our personal energy grounds into the energetic matrix of our immediate environment.

Overall, the entire body functions as a fractal expression of electromagnetic energy. You are, quite literally, an energy being with a liquid crystal interior, incased in skin, with three divine energy centers and two personal ones.

The key to understanding yourself as an embodiment of God is to understand your energetic nature, just as the key to understanding physical reality is to understand the energetic structures that comprise the physical world. Your primary concern as an energetic bio-vehicle for God to enjoy reality in is this: Am I being aware and authentic with the energy that is me? If you can honestly answer yes to that question, then that is all you need ever do.

This view is at odds with virtually all religious traditions, especially the Western Monotheistic traditions. These traditions have invented concepts like souls, sin, morality, and salvation and damnation. These concepts have no basis in reality and have nothing whatsoever to do with your bio-vehicle or how it actually functions.

Key Ideas

- Your body is a "vehicle" for God to enjoy reality in
- Your personality is the natural expression of your energy as an embodiment of God
- Human bodies have three "divine" energy centers: consciousness/the brain and nervous system; the heart, lungs, and vascular system; the genitals and reproductive system
- Human bodies have two "personal" energy centers: the throat and mouth; the stomach and digestive system
- Egos block the natural expression of the energy radiating from your divine energy centers whenever you fail to express your energy authentically
- Authentic energy flow has nothing to do with moralistic systems of behavior

Actual Energy vs. Imaginary "Subtle" Energy

It should be clear by this point in the discussion that the kinds of energies and energy centers in the body that are being described here have nothing whatsoever to do with obscure mystical ideas of "subtle" energy. Many religious and cultural traditions teach about "subtle" energy and "subtle bodies." For example, we have the *chakra* system of both Hinduism and Buddhism, and we have the meridians and chi of Taoism. It might be tempting to compare these ideas of energy to the discussion of energy as provided in this guide. This would be fundamentally misguided, however, and it should be made clear that *there is no relationship between the ideas presented here and religious constructions of "subtle" energy.*

The difference should be immediately clear. The energy being discussed here is the energy of our actual physiological system – our brains and nervous system, our hearts and circulatory system, our sexual organs and evolutionary transformation. In other words, this is *your actual body.* There is nothing "subtle" about this.

On the other hand, Buddhists and Hindus are quite explicit when they proclaim that your *chakras* are your "subtle" energy system and this system *is not necessarily correlated with your physiological system*, which would be characterized as a "gross" system (as opposed to "subtle"). This distinction is obvious when gurus describe how you have *chakras* above your head and below your anus: this has nothing to do with your actual physical body.

Let's make the distinction even more obvious. Imagine that your car is having engine trouble. You take it to the mechanic's shop and are greeted by two mechanics. One mechanic asks you how your car is running and then proceeds to open up the hood and tinker with the engine. The other mechanic, however, never bothers to look at the engine. Instead, he pulls out some books with pictures of cars that show different wheels of colored energy with different symbols and syllables and starts to discourse on how your car can be made to run better if these energy centers can only be properly opened up, purified, and activated.

Who do you think is actually going to fix your car - the "real" mechanic who is concerned about the actual machinery of your vehicle, or the mechanic who wants to talk about these mysterious energy centers that seem only vaguely related to your actual car?

To put it bluntly, the kinds of energy being discussed in this guide *have nothing to do with any concept of subtle energy and are not comparable to religious constructions of subtle energy in any way.* Subtle energy is imaginary. Real energy is physiological.

Life and Death

Perhaps the most difficult concept for people to accept is that the entheological model of God, life, and reality that is being articulated here indicates that any notion of an "afterlife" is a complete fantasy.

God is life. God is *your life.* You, as a vehicle for God to experience reality in, are dependent on your vehicle/body in order for you to have your personal perspective as a character that God is playing. Without your body, you have no "personal" perspective as one manifestation of the multi-being. The conclusion is therefore obvious: when your vehicle is gone, so is your personal perspective.

In a sense, your perspective as an individual is a gift from God. The gift only lasts as long as the vehicle does. God, as the multi-being, is able to occupy all perspectives simultaneously. As an individual expression of God in a body, you have *your perspective.* That is your gift of experiencing yourself as an individual.

So what happens at death? Is there life after death? Is there a heaven or a hell or reincarnation? Is there reward or punishment?

Ultimately, nothing that any religion has ever claimed about these questions or their answers is relevant. It is all pure fantasy and ego projection. When your body is gone, that unique perspective that was "you" is gone. God lives on eternally. God has billions more bodies and perspectives to enjoy. Your perspective was just one perspective in the grand evolutionary arc of life and at your death is then simply gone.

Think of it this way, if you like: God is playing a big, complex video game. "You" are a character in that game. When your character dies in the game, it's the end of that character. That doesn't affect the gamer (God) at all, because God just gets more new characters. Similarly, when you dream, you dream all kinds of characters, even yourself. However, you are all the characters, not just the one you identify your personal perspective with.

So no, there is no "life after death." There is nowhere for "you" to go, because *you are already there*. There is no state of purification to be achieved. No enlightenment to gain. No tests of character or spirit to be overcome. Nothing. You are a character in a complex game. Your *only* task is to be authentic to your character and nothing else. Given that this is the *only* time that you have as this character, your job is to make the most out of it while your character is around. Everything else about what you should or shouldn't do, especially when one is getting advice from religions, is pure ego projection and fantasy with no bearing on reality at all.

This also means that there is no reincarnation and no karma, so the Eastern religions don't fare much better than the Western Monotheistic traditions when it comes to describing true reality. The *only one* who "reincarnates" is God, who is the life and consciousness already present in every living being. There is no such thing as an individual consciousness or spirit or soul that can reincarnate, and since there is no such thing, there also is no such thing as karma (cause and effect accumulated over lifetimes of choices and behavior). It is *not* your individual consciousness that evolves over many lifetimes. It is God that is evolving as *all living beings simultaneously*. Our evolution is *collective, not individual, because we are the collective. We are that one being*.

A startling conclusion is that there is no reason to follow what any religion says about what one *should* or *should not do*. It all becomes a matter of choice. Religions can present you with options for how you *may want to behave*, but none of their moral, ethical, or metaphysical rationales for the views they promote hold up under scrutiny. For example, Buddhism teaches you should be a vegetarian because eating animals causes bad karma and a bad rebirth, thereby lessening your chances of reaching enlightenment. But, since there is no reincarnation, nor karma, the only *real* reason to be a vegetarian is if you personally want to. None of the metaphysical reasons given by Buddhism for vegetarianism hold up when considering the true nature of reality.

It is much the same case with Christianity. This religion teaches that certain behaviors are sins and will prevent you from entering heaven and will damn your soul. Well, you don't have a soul, so there's nothing to save or damn. If you want to "be a good Christian," that is up to you, but don't expect anything for it. God does not have any reward for you.

However, this is not to say that religions don't have some good advice for living your life. Buddhism teaches compassion and Christianity turning the other cheek and loving your neighbors. You *will* lead a happier life by following good advice, but that doesn't mean that it has anything to do with God, the afterlife, or what comes next. It is only good advice if it helps you remain clear, centered, and authentic in the present moment (in which case, Buddhism fares far better than most religions in terms of practical advice, given its attention to remaining present and focused and its emphasis on cultivating awareness through meditation).

Given that worrying about life after death is a specious issue, *anything* that draws your attention away from living authentically in the present moment is a diversion and most probably an ego-generated illusion. If you want to have a goal for yourself to help you on your path to becoming healthier, happier and more centered and less trapped by fear and negative thoughts and emotions, then I strongly suggest that you get clear on who and what you are and be present with yourself and your energy in every moment. Ultimately, this is a simple task with many monumental challenges.

The remainder of this guide will share with you how *you can do it!*

Key Ideas

- Your energy system is related to your physiology and is not "subtle" energy – it is electromagnetic energy
- The direct source of your energy is God
- Souls and spirits and subtle bodies are religious concepts that have no correlate in actual reality
- Concepts of an afterlife and all related moral systems are a fantasy and have no relation to actual reality
- Your life and consciousness is God in embodied form: there are no intermediaries

How to Begin

Waking Up

I like to think of it this way: What we experience as normal reality is God's altered state. In God's baseline state, all things are one and there is no separation. However, in ordinary reality, we experience things as separate all the time and most of us have no idea that we're actually God and all of what we experience is ourselves. In other words, when we humans are in our "normal state," we, as God, are fundamentally confused about the nature of our existence. We are confusing all kinds of fantasies and illusions with reality and we think that there are a bunch of separate beings running around, all doing their thing. We are God's altered state!

Conversely, when we alter our state of consciousness, we can get closer to the baseline state that is pure God consciousness. From my personal experience, this is best achieved through the ingestion of 5-MeO-DMT and is far more effective than any meditation regimen or other "mystical" practice. 5-MeO-DMT is about as altered as any human being can get, but from the God perspective, that state of consciousness is simply the way things actually are. In other words, that state of consciousness of complete mystical union is actually the super-mundane state of reality. It's the most ordinary, non-fantastical thing. It's the reality game that we're playing here in embodied form that is fantastical, given that it's all a complex and grand illusion.

But don't be mistaken. Just because reality is an illusion that doesn't mean it isn't "real." This is as "real" as it gets. For this reason, no matter if one wakes up to the true nature of reality or not, one must always be concerned with protecting the vehicle. It doesn't matter how awakened you are – if you walk in front of a semi moving at 70 mph, it's going to cream your body all over the freeway – that's simply the way the reality game works. If you want to stick around to be able to enjoy your personal perspective, then you will always protect your vehicle for as long as you are playing the reality game. The game is *much* more fun when you can avoid unnecessary pain and suffering!

Waking up to the true nature of your being means essentially only one thing, and that is liberation from the confines of your ego, thereby letting yourself be more fully yourself and more responsible for your personal experience of the reality game. Waking up does *not* mean developing paranormal powers or anything mystical or mystifying at all. It simply means liberating yourself from your ego and thereby living a happier and more satisfying life. It doesn't mean you'll be able to "manifest" anything you want, or "create your own reality," as are popular beliefs among New Age aficionados. Nor does it mean developing psychic powers as Buddhism and Hinduism claim. And it *especially* does not mean developing an ability to travel in astral realms or visit alien civilizations or any such fantastical nonsense. Waking up is simply about being fully present and authentic with your energy at all times and is best described as being energetically open. When you can do that, your ego will no longer have a hold on you. When your ego no longer has a hold on you, you won't be taken in by fantasy and ego-projection. You won't engage with others' self-created dramas and power-plays and you'll understand how to avoid making ones of your own. You will be happier and you will feel supreme love for yourself and for God (which are one and the same). You will be at peace.

But you will still be in the reality game until your vehicle is no more, and at that point, you personally have nothing to worry about, because you, as God, live on, and will continue in perfect self-love forever.

Not a bad deal, is it?

Are you ready to take responsibility and be yourself?

Taking Stock

Before beginning the process of opening yourself to the full expression of your energy, it is good to take stock and see where you currently are. Consider some preliminary questions:

- Do you feel that you authentically express yourself and your feelings, or do you hold back and restrain yourself?

- If you restrain yourself, what is your rationale? Family? Friends? Culture? Religion?

- Do you find that you judge others and yourself?

- Where do these judgments come from?

- Do you ever engage in behavior patterns that you know are not beneficial to yourself or others but can't seem to break out of the negative patterns?

- Do you feel that you are a victim in life?

- Do you indulge in self-pity?

- Do you feel personally under attack when people criticize views or beliefs that you hold?

- Are you honest with yourself at all times?

- Are you honest with others, even when being so is challenging for others?

- Do you face your fears with love and acceptance or do you prefer to do combat with them and try and eliminate them?

- Do you always stay in your comfort zone or do you push your edges to discover your potential?

- Are you satisfied with the level of communication, trust, and love in your intimate relationships?

- Is what others think of you a major motivating factor in your life?

Exercise 1

Take the time to think honestly about your answers to these questions. You might find it helpful to spend some time writing your responses down on paper and see what patterns develop. As you see patterns emerge, you can start to ask youself, "What could I do in this situation to take more responsibility for myself?" For example, write out some situations where you indulged in self-pity. What were the circumstances? How did you feel? What did you do at the time? Now, ask yourself, how could you have taken more responsibility for your reactions and emotions in that situation? What could you have done to express yourself more authentically? What expectations were you attached to that, when they didn't materialize as you hoped, led to your feelings of self-pity.

Keep in mind that *how you respond to any situation is always your choice.* Shit happens. That can't be avoided, but how you respond to any situation and how you mobilize your energy is *always your personal responsibility.* If you can master that, then you can master your life. It doesn't mean that you are in control of anything outside of your immediate vehicle and your immediate consciousness, but it does mean that you become in control of yourself, rather than letting your confused ego run the show.

In short, this is all about self-mastery.

Exercise 2

For another exercise, take a look at what it means for you to be authentic with yourself. Take a piece of paper and divide it in half. On one side, write down everything you can associate with the feeling of being authentic, honest, and true to yourself. Then on the other side, write down everything you associate with feeling inauthentic, dishonest and untrue. Try to write freely without any attachment or judgment with anything that comes up. This is not about right or wrong thinking. This is about looking honestly at your current thoughts and feelings.

How do you feel about your lists of associations? Which feels more attractive to you? Without judging yourself in any way, but being honest, where are you more of the time mentally, emotionally, consciously, etc. Are you on the authentic side or the inauthentic side? Remember, it's OK if your honest assessment shows you that you're not where you want to be. Don't judge yourself. Just recognize that this is where you currently are and give yourself the goal of taking more control of yourself and increasing your personal responsibility.

Exercise 3

Perhaps the most important question is this: Do you love yourself fully, completely, and unconditionally? Try answering this question verbally. How does your answer feel as it comes out of your body and vibrates the air around you? Does your answer sound true to you? Does it *feel* true? Is there doubt or hesitation or qualification in your voice? Or is it pure, rich, and resonate with the profound energetic qualities of truth? You might even want to record your voice in answering this question. Listen to your recording at different times and see what new perspectives you have on your own truth. You can even record your answer many times over a course of days, weeks, months or years. Listen to all your answers and see what's changing as you get more in touch with yourself and as you take more responsibility. You'll be surprised at how the quality of your tone and voice changes. The further along you get on your path, the less like "you" your original answer will sound.

Exercise 4

Another exercise to help you take stock is to complete the sentence of, "I am . . ."

At the top of the piece of paper, write the words "I am" in clear, bold letters. Then take 10-15 minutes to fill the page with as many free associations as you can. Remember not to judge anything that you write. This is not about right or wrong associations. For example, if you feel depressed, then write that down. Don't censor yourself by telling yourself "I know I shouldn't be depressed so I won't write that."

Just be honest! And don't be idealistic, either. For example, if you don't actually feel that you are God, don't write it! This is about discovering what you actually feel, not what you think you should feel.

When you are done, circle everything that you perceive as positive on the page in one color and circle everything you perceive as negative in another color. Don't do anything with it. Just observe what has come up. Set the paper aside. When you feel ready, perhaps in a few days, weeks, or months, do this exercise again. Get out your original answers and compare them to your new answers. What has shifted? Has the balance between positive and negative shifted, or is it the same? If it has shifted, what do you feel you are doing differently to produce different results? Can you identify healthy, authentic patterns developing in your behavior? Remember, when doing this exercise it is very important that you only focus on how you feel right then, while doing the exercise. Your goal is to provide a current snapshot of where you are at energetically, emotionally and mentally. It is not about cataloging everything you've been through over the past week. It is about getting in touch with yourself in the current moment.

As a normal human being, it is quite likely that in doing these exercises you will find some areas in your life and in your behavior where you are not being honest, authentic, and true to yourself. This is good. Awareness is the first step. Taking stock is not about giving your ego fuel to punish yourself or judge yourself. Your ego will likely want to step in and say, "See, you *should do this, you should be this way.*" Don't listen to your ego. It's just trying to take control. Taking stock is not about what *should be*. It is about finding out *what actually is*.

Exercise 5

For this exercise, at the top of a piece of paper, write in big, bold letters, "GOD." Write everything you can think of that you associate with this word. It's OK if you're an atheist or agnostic. Write whatever comes to mind. Again, there are no right or wrong answers here. Take about 10 – 15 minutes.

After you are done with your list, read through what you've written without adding anything. Looking honestly at what you've done, how would you characterize your list? Do you find expression of fear, judgment and doubt, or do you find love, peace and acceptance? Does it seem realistic to you or not? How does your list make you feel?

If you are unsure how your list makes you feel, try reading your list authentically and recording your voice. For example, if something on your list makes you feel sarcastic or cynical, let yourself read that item in a cynical or sarcastic tone. If something makes you feel mocking, then read it in a mocking tone. If something on your list makes you want to sing, then sing it. Your goal is not to sound how you *think* you should sound but rather to let your sounds match how you actually feel. Listen to your recording. How does your pitch and tone of voice change with the different items on your list? What qualities do you hear in your voice? Do you hear authenticity?

You can repeat this exercise as many times as you like and observe what changes, what stays the same, and where authenticity, trust and confidence grow or diminish. It's never about right or wrong answers. It is about taking an honest look in the mirror to learn how you actually feel.

The Mirror

Ultimately, awakening to reality and opening yourself energetically is really just a process of looking into the mirror of who and what you actually are. As you remove your resistance to the energy of your being, the mirror will become clearer. As you overcome your illusions and fantasies, you will find that the mirror distorts less and less. Eventually, if you persist and let go of your ego and your remaining resistance, you will see your true self, God, reflected in every aspect of your experience at all times and all moments, for God is the only thing that truly exists, and it is you.

All of reality is a mirror. The question for you personally is this: Do you want to play like a child in the funhouse of distorted mirrors, or do you want to be an adult and see your reflection clearly, free of any illusion and distortion?

If you want to be an adult, then it is up to you to take responsibility for learning to recognize yourself in the mirror. No one can do it for you. No savior is coming to lead the way or hold your hand. No amount of faith, belief, worship, or prayer will ever do it. No priest, guru, or shaman can do it for you. There is no grand cosmic awakening coming that will do the work for you. If you want to wake up, then it is your responsibility and yours alone. If you are ready, then the time is now. Your personal life in this body is short. Take advantage of it while you can. *You only have one chance.* It will be challenging, but as someone who has taken the leap, I assure you, it is the greatest thing you can ever do for yourself or anyone else. Let go of your fear and gaze into the mirror of who and what you truly are. You are more profoundly beautiful, powerful, and loving than your ego can possibly imagine.

YOU ARE GOD!

The Preliminaries of Practice

The most effective tools for opening your awareness to your true energetic nature are entheogens, or substances that "generate the experience of God within." However, there is a great deal that can be done without entheogens that can help with the process of awakening. Before turning the discussion to entheogens, let's address some of these preliminary practices first.

Meditation

Meditation is a powerful tool to help you gain some mastery over the vagaries of the mind. Learning techniques of maintaining focus, concentration, and awareness can be extremely helpful in navigating the experiences of altered states of consciousness that entheogens open one up to. Many people, especially in the modern world, find maintaining focus and concentration for any length of time to be extraordinarily challenging as these skills are largely atrophied in our high-paced, instant gratification, multi-tasking and sensory overload culture. Our culture is filled with diversions, distractions, and temptations to draw you away from the present moment of what actually is. Meditation, on the other hand, teaches you how to slow down, set your busy thoughts aside, and simply pay attention and be present. This is an invaluable skill and sorely needed in the modern world.

There are many different meditation traditions. Some come with more dogma, symbolism, metaphysics and religious fantasy than others. Zen meditation is particularly sparse and unencumbered by religious ritual or metaphysics, and I therefore suggest this as a good place to begin. Zen meditation is simply about sitting, breathing, and being present. Nothing more, and nothing less. Such a practice can be easier to work into than, say, *tantric* meditation, which teaches all kinds of *mudras*, *mantras*, visualization, prayers, rituals, and use of complex symbolism, etc. In more "complex" meditation traditions, it is very difficult to get into the practice without having to learn and accept the entire corpus of religious beliefs and propositions, many of which are ego-produced fantasies, speculations, and metaphysics. One does not need to be a Buddhist to practice Zen meditation, however. Anyone can sit and follow their breath. No religion required!

The primary goal of meditation is to let your mind function naturally without being attached to any of your thoughts and feelings. It is a practice in maintaining mindful awareness without attachment or expectation. It is a great way to get in touch with what is really going on inside your mind and become aware of just how busy your internal dialogue actually is. Even sitting quietly for five minutes is nearly impossible for some people, at least at first. Be patient with yourself and give yourself the time you need to ease into your practice and become comfortable with observing your mind, thoughts, and feelings.

Your goal in meditating is to always bring yourself back to the present moment. When your thoughts start to project out into the future, bring them back to your breath in the present. When your thoughts run to what occurred in the past, bring them back to your breath once more. When stories and fantasies start to arise in your mind, let go of them and come back to the present. Meditating is not about figuring things out or telling stories to yourself. It is simply about being present, here and now.

Getting in Touch with Your Body and Energy

There are many ways you can get in touch with your body and your energy in everyday life. Dance, martial arts, yoga, sports, gymnastics, making love, etc., are all viable methods for being in your body. To really get in touch with your energy, however, it is important that you incorporate expressive action into your body movements. For example, becoming a professional dancer is different that letting your body move to the music any way that feels right and good for you. When your aim is to get in touch with your body and energy it is useful to keep in mind that it is not about performing any specific actions correctly or artfully. It is about letting yourself move authentically and expressively. There is no right or wrong in authentic, expressive action.

For example, try putting on some music that you like when you are home alone. Stand or sit in the middle of the room. Don't "try" and dance any way in particular. In fact, don't try and do anything at all. You can sit or stand still until you feel inspired to move. Then just let yourself follow your energy. It isn't about looking good or impressing anyone. It's just about letting the energy flow and following it with your body.

Vocalizing

A primary medium through which humans express their energy is with their voice. Thus, another way to get comfortable with your energy is to get comfortable with using your voice to express yourself.

This can take all kinds of forms, from prayer, chanting, singing, to just making sounds and noises. Give yourself opportunities throughout the day to simply express yourself verbally/vocally. It doesn't matter what comes out. Just do it!

Try experimenting. If you are a soft-spoken person, try being loud. If you are usually boisterous, try subtle manipulations of sound. Search for what feels authentic for you. Don't be concerned about sounding like anyone or anything in particular. Just make some sound!

To really have fun, I suggest learning some throat or overtone singing as these forms of vocal expression mobilize a great deal of energy, are fun to do, and sound great!

Bodywork

Tensions, stresses and energetic blocks and wounds are carried in the body. As you begin to unwind yourself, you may find that getting bodywork and massages help to release all of the blocked energy you've been carrying around. If you are new to bodywork, you will probably find that getting a massage comes with all kinds of emotional releases. When the body worker finds the right spot on your back, for example, you might start to cry or laugh uncontrollably without knowing why. The why is not important. Just let yourself feel it and express it. Give yourself permission to unwind and release whatever energy is not serving you. Given that most people hold back on expressing themselves, most people do have energy to release, even if they don't realize it. Bodywork is a great way to help that energy get out without having to consciously find and release it.

Self-expression

Regardless of whether you feel you have any artistic or musical skill or not, finding a way to express yourself creatively is enormously helpful in getting in touch with yourself and your energy. Expressing yourself is not about good or bad, it is about the process and experience of expressing. You don't have to be "good" at painting to express yourself through painting, for example. Anyone can pick up a paintbrush and apply paint to canvas. Just do it! Don't be attached to form or outcome. It will be fun and possibly cathartic. Artistic expression is all about self-discovery and the process of creating, not the end product. So let yourself be an artist and express yourself without judgment.

The Open Heart

Ultimately, being open to your energy means keeping an open heart. We close our hearts when we feel threatened or when we experience fear or judgment. Given that the vast majority of what threatens us or gives us fear or judgment is ego-projection, our egos are our own worst enemies when it comes to keeping our hearts open. A general maxim, which may seem overwhelming at first, is to love all equally without any exception. If you can maintain that attitude, then you can keep your heart open.

This does not mean that you have to actively experience love for all things at all moments – that would be a fairly large task. What it does mean is that you should practice giving love to everything and everyone you encounter at any given moment. This is much more manageable than trying to love everything all at once. It just means loving what you experience, yourself, and others, in each moment. For example, it doesn't mean that you have to actively love all 6.5 billion people on the planet. Rather, just love whoever is with you, and if no one is with you, then just love yourself. And keep in mind, love is truth, so loving whoever you are with means being honest and truthful with them, even if it makes them uncomfortable. Love is definitely *not* indulging in the fantasies and illusions of others. Love is about living in truth.

People want to close off their hearts when they feel wounded. They become a victim and then indulge in self-pity. They make excuses for why they can't keep their heart open. Despite the fact that pain hurts, people indulge in it all the time. It validates the illusions of the ego and gives it strength. It is a way of running away from taking responsibility for oneself. It is easier to identify others as the source of our suffering than to own up to our own energy and take responsibility for our own thoughts and emotions. The open heart is the heart that takes responsibility for itself and its own happiness. It does not rely upon others and gives love freely and unconditionally. The open heart is godly for God gives love continually and unconditionally from an infinite supply. The open heart will never exhaust itself.

Spending Time in Nature

Nature is an excellent place for self-reflection – literally. This is especially true for natural areas that have been undisturbed by humans and that have no introduced species. In such areas, one can experience the energetic structures of nature in their "natural" form. While a garden or park can provide an enjoyable nature experience, undisturbed nature is a more accurate representation of how energy works when left to its own devices. Patterns and colors blend together or accent each other. Flows of rock, dirt, water, ice, and sand mark out their fractal patterns. Plants grow in intricate fractal geometry to convert sunlight into useable energy for other living beings. All of nature is a constantly moving canvas of multiple energetic patterns working simultaneously across multiple levels, all in cohesion and concert with each other. Nature is simply energy at work, being itself.

Given that God is nature and that you are God, you are also nature. For this reason, undisturbed nature shows you the natural patterns of energy that ultimately are all a part of you. Observing transformations and patterns in nature gives insight into how energy works. It helps center one's personal energy and relax the anxieties of the ego-based mind. When done solitarily, it is also a refreshing escape from the games of other egos.

Personally, I recommend taking as much solitary or quite time in undisturbed nature as possible. It is beautiful, it makes you feel good, and it is a pure reflection. It is also a great place to start before engaging in any work with entheogenic medicines.

Key Ideas

- Get to know yourself before undertaking entheogenic practice
- Use bodywork, meditation, dance, and time in nature to center yourself and gain intimate knowledge of how you feel
- Aside from work with entheogens, spending time in undisturbed nature provides the best mirror to reflect with
- Explore ways to express yourself

PART III

OPENING TO ENERGY WITH ENTHEOGENS

ENTHEOGENIC PRACTICE

Working with the Medicines

We are now ready to address what it means to work with the visionary medicines, or entheogens, and how they can serve your awakening to your infinite energy.

First, there is the question of legality. The reality is that the majority of truly effective visionary plants and substances are illegal to posses and use. Most governments equate *any* use of entheogens with abuse and only very rarely make legal exceptions for religious practitioners. I have written extensively on this topic elsewhere, so I have no intention of delving deeply into this problem here, other than to say that the prohibition against using entheogens is a fundamental violation of your right as an embodiment of God to explore your own nature. As far as I am personally concerned, no government or authority as *any* right to prohibit anyone from freely exploring their own mind in ways that do no harm to others.

The situation is also bizarrely absurd. DMT is illegal to possess and use in most countries, with some exceptions for religions that use ayahuasca as a ceremonial sacrament (which contains DMT). However, as has already been pointed out, DMT is a primary ingredient in mammalian evolution and is already present in every single mammal on this planet, including every human. It is also found in countless species of plants and mushrooms (in the form of psilocin and psilocybin). How in the world can something that is *naturally in our bodies at all times be an illegal substance?* As a human being, you are, by your very biology, possessing and using DMT *right now!* By our current drug laws, every single person on this planet should be arrested and thrown in jail for possessing and using DMT. This situation is bizarre.

As of writing this, in the U.S., 5-MeO-DMT, perhaps the most profound entheogenic substance on the planet, is currently under consideration for Schedule I status as an illegal drug. As with DMT, 5-MeO-DMT is already in every human being on the planet. It is as natural to us as breathing air or drinking water and we cannot live without it. It is a fundamental part of what makes us human. And now the government wants to make it illegal.

What in the world is going on here? Does this actually make sense to anyone? How can natural compounds already found within the human body be illegal? For that matter, how can *any* part of nature be made illegal? Isn't that the equivalent to outlawing God?

Ah . . . foolish mortals . . .

So, virtually anyone who wants to explore their energetic nature through the use of entheogens runs the risk of imprisonment, with few exceptions. The absurdity is profound. You can be thrown in jail for taking the responsibility of getting clear on who and what you actually are as an energetic being and embodiment of God. Using natural compounds to explore your divinity is a crime. It is a startling reality check for anyone who thinks they live in a "free" country.

Are Entheogens *really* the most effective tool for Awakening?

When it comes to awakening to your true energetic nature as a fractal energy being, entheogens, and particularly the tryptamines, are the most effective tools available to humanity. There is nothing more reliable and consistent for opening your perception of yourself and your experience to the reality of energy as entheogens. While other techniques of altering consciousness and perception can be experientially effective, especially with sustained practice, there really is no comparison. You can spend a lifetime meditating and not get much more out of it than a sore bottom and tingly legs from cutting off your circulation. All it takes is one hit of 5-MeO-DMT and in about 10 seconds you'll have the most profound energetic opening of your life that will surpass anything you have ever experienced in meditation by infinite light years. It is simply a matter of effectiveness.

Another way of looking at the situation is this: You can try and map out the heavens with your naked eye, or you can look through the Hubble telescope. Entheogens are the Hubble telescope of the inner world. Sure, you can look at the sky with your naked eyes, but why not use the Hubble if it is right there and you have access to it? What would be the point of doing it with your naked eyes? So your ego can be proud that you "did it" on "your own?"

Personally, I have yet to meet anyone who has been able to honestly say that their meditation practice has gotten them to the same states that can be achieved with entheogens. Regardless of one's meditation practice, I've never seen anyone experience 5-MeO-DMT and say, "that's just like my meditation." In fact, it's the opposite. People proclaim that they never could have imagined the sheer beauty and completeness of the 5-MeO-DMT experience and that nothing in their mediation practice has ever come close to such a total and radical experience of oneness with the true energy of being. As a tool for exploring consciousness and one's energetic nature, 5-meO-DMT is simply incomparable.

However, once one becomes experienced with entheogenic states of consciousness, then these states can be achieved without any entheogens. You have to know what you are looking for, in a sense, in order to find it again. For example, after experiencing 5-MeO-DMT, one's personal mediation practice can become profoundly more powerful and effective, but without that initial introduction, it is extremely difficult for anyone to reach a full-blown 5-MeO-DMT state on their own (and remember that 5-MeO-DMT is a natural neurotransmitter already present in your body). Once you've had the introduction, you can start to actualize the endogenous 5-MeO-DMT in your body and produce endogenous releases, but you need to know what that feels like in order to cultivate it.

Another advantage to working with entheogens is that they put you directly in touch with your own energetic nature without any intermediaries. Remember that all of reality is a mirror, but many of the individual mirrors walking around out there are distorted by their egos and their illusions and fantasies. In other words, working with others to find clarity in yourself is challenging as there is no guarantee that those you are working with are clear themselves. For example, working with a guru can be great help in deepening your meditation, but if that guru is filling you with ideas of karma and reincarnation and subtle energy bodies and astral projection, then you are working with a distorted mirror, let alone trying to deal with your own distorted mirror.

Entheogens cut out the middleman, so to speak. Entheogens put you directly in touch with yourself as God and the only distorted ego mirror you have to deal with in such a context is your own. Dealing with one distorted mirror is far easier than dealing with two, or many. Given that the *true nature of reality exists within you*, the most effective route to getting clear on what that reality is is to dive within yourself to discover it for yourself. And given that the true nature of reality is energetic, if you want to understand reality, you have to understand energy.

When it comes to opening your perception and experience to the reality of energy that exists within you, there is nothing more effective than entheogens. It's just that simple. There is no need to get tangled up in moralistic or religious arguments about "drugs" or "cheating" or anything of that sort. Entheogens are simply tools, and as tools, they are the most effective at what they do. A hallmark of clear intelligence is using the proper tool for the job. Why not use the best tools available?

Lastly, given that all of reality is one, and all things are God, could it really be an "accident" that entheogens affect us the way that they do? That seems profoundly unlikely. Rather, there would seem to be a reason why entheogens affect us they way they do: God created crystal keys to help unlock consciousness in its vehicles so that they can come to understand the true nature of their being and the reality in which they live. Entheogens are crystal keys that unlock the doors to the Divine Imagination.

Cautions

Working with entheogens is serious business and should not be taken lightly. It takes dedication and often a tremendous amount of bravery and personal perseverance. It is by *no means an easy path.* Overcoming the illusions and fears of your ego and accepting your true nature as God is the most significant challenge you could ever possibly embark upon as a human being. However, given that you already are

God, you can rest assured that *you can do it!* Ultimately, there is nothing to be achieved and nothing gained. *You already are fully awakened as God.* Thus, working with entheogens is not about achieving some exalted or rarified state (as is promoted by meditation traditions) but rather is about letting go of your resistance and relaxing fully into the core of your true energetic nature. But remember: your ego is designed to convince you that you are a separate being. That is its function. To awaken to your true nature, you *must* transcend your ego. Your ego will never go away, but by transcending it, you can release yourself from its grip. Yet within this process, your ego will use *every resource at its disposal to keep you trapped in self-generated illusions*. In the end, it is as simple as relaxing out of your ego and being true to your energy, but getting there can be profoundly challenging.

Thus, if you choose to embark on a process of self-discovery with entheogens, be prepared for a difficult ride. Opening yourself up to your own personal mirror of the divine can be terrifying and the *only* way through is to confront your fears and illusions. Really, it is a process of letting yourself "die" fully in order to discover your true nature. You will have to find the strength and courage within yourself to willingly participate in this radical process if you truly want to awaken and open energetically.

This process is also profoundly beautiful and personally satisfying, as well, so it isn't all difficulty. The entire point of seeking personal awakening is to find happiness, authenticity, and personal fulfillment by living in truth. These rewards are well worth any difficulties or challenges one might face along the way. This is the motivation for undertaking this great work. And let's be clear: *if everyone took the responsibility to awaken to the true nature of reality, this would be a profoundly different world.* Just imagine what the world would be like if *everyone* let go of their illusions, fears, and ego-generated drama games. War, violence, manipulation, exploitation, and human-produced suffering would be a thing of the past. It is absolutely true that world peace and global harmony begins with each individual. If you want to do your part to make this world a better place, then it all begins with *you*.

Things to be Aware of

Attachment to Story

A common effect of working with entheogens is attachment to story. People see visions or encounter other "beings" and then proceed to weave fantastic stories around their experiences. Terence McKenna and the infamous machine elves are an excellent case in point. Terence "encountered" the machine elves in a now-notorious DMT trip and subsequently created an entire cultural mythology around these ephemeral beings. As will be explained below in the discussion of the Divine Imagination, Terence was unable to recognize himself in the mirror and thus became attached to the idea of machine elves, which dovetailed nicely into his fantasy of UFO's, intergalactic space travel, and 2012. *All of this is story*, and subsequently, fantasy.

Another classic example of attachment to story comes from the modern religion of Santo Daime. The founder of the Daime experienced a vision of the "Queen of the Forest" coming to him and telling him that he was a reincarnation of John the Baptist, and he was to reinstate the Doctrine of Jesus through the Daime (a version of the ayahuasca drink). Once again, we see someone who fails to recognize himself in the mirror, gets attached to ideas of entities and reincarnation, and then uses that as motivation to create a modern religious mythology of the Daime. Another story is born . . .

The solution is quite simple: don't become attached to story! Working with entheogens can be like going to see a movie that has been personally designed just for you. Enjoy the movie, but don't get attached to it. It's just a movie, after all! Another way of putting this is to remember not to take visions literally. They are symbol and metaphor, not ontological reality.

Your job is to stay present in the moment. Story is the exact opposite of this. Story takes a span of time and turns it into an object of attachment. Story has *nothing* to do with the present moment. Any focus on story is *always* a distraction from the present. It does not serve you, so let it go.

The Dangers of Shamanism

Many people who work with entheogens desire to do so in a shamanic context or under the guidance of an experienced shaman. It is important to keep in mind, however, the dangers that come with shamanic practice. Shamanism, in contrast to the ideas presented in this guide, is pluralistic, meaning that shamanic cultures traditionally teach that the universe is comprised of multiple spirits residing in multiple realms – basically the opposite of the radical non-dualism being presented here. Within such shamanic systems there is widespread projection and reinforcement of ideas of separation. In turn, shamanic cultures tend to exhibit high degrees of jealousy, envy, fear, and anxiety. The universe is split into realms of good and bad spirits and good and bad shamans. The shamans fight with the spirits and fight with each other. Sorcery is thrown back and forth and people work "dark magic." It's all illusion, but when egos are playing the game, they don't know its illusion and react to it as though it were real.

People who become involved in shamanism often find that they are overly concerned about "picking up bad energy" from people or places. They engage in "protective" practices to try and shield themselves from others. They go to shamans to have "bad spirits" removed or "retrieve their lost soul." While these practices can make someone feel better and even improve their health, it's a bit of a catch-22, because they are willingly engaging in the ego-fantasy and illusion generated by shamanic cultures.

Consider an example: A person is feeling troubled by their patterns of behavior that do not seem to serve their highest good and they want to address it so they go see a shaman. The shaman divines that the person is possessed by an evil spirit that is manipulating this person's choices and behaviors and prescribes an ayahuasca session to release the demon. The person is now fearful that there is something "bad" that needs to "taken out" and is dependent on the shaman to accomplish this for them. The shaman and patient then drink ayahuasca. The patient then starts to feel the struggle inside and gives more and more energy to the "demon" and it truly does start to feel like an entity of its own. The shaman then performs ritual extraction techniques and the patient energetically feels something "being released" through the actions of the shaman. Case closed, patient better.

The problem is that there are no such things as spirits or entities that can "attach" themselves to you or possess you. Any such "entity" or "energy" is merely a part of yourself that you are not personally taking responsibility for. A shamanic extraction process "exteriorizes" your internal conflict and then attempts to banish it. However, if you haven't addressed the underlying irresponsibility and disowning of your own energy, then you are merely perpetuating your personal illusion and you lay the groundwork for it to return at any time because you haven't properly faced and owned it as yourself. In other words, this shamanic process is engaging in story and attachment to ideas of separation. It is a fantasy game. That's fine, if you want to live in fantasy and accept the consequences of doing so (fear, judgment, inauthenticity, etc.), but if you want to live in reality, this is not helpful.

Fear of Losing Control

When people work with entheogens, particularly high-level entheogens such as extracted or synthetic DMT or 5-MeO-DMT, spontaneous experiences become common. This is especially true with 5-MeO-DMT. It is not unusual for a person who has experienced 5-MeO-DMT to awaken every night for a week or so thereafter finding themselves fully launched into a psychedelic experience. This can be *extraordinarily unnerving*. People might also start to spontaneously see visions and scenes or psychedelic imagery when they are falling asleep.

The important thing to remember here is simply to let go and relax. Spontaneous experiences tend to mellow out, over time, if one can relax about it. Reacting with fear and anxiety will only make the situation worse. The problem is that energy and perception are always moving and changing. A common fear is "I'm never going to come back," but everyone always does. So trust in that and just relax if these experiences start to happen to you. Don't try and fight them. Just accept that you're opening to your energy and remember that energy is always moving and changing. No state of being or experience is permanent.

It is also important to remain vigilant about not becoming attached to story in such experiences as well. If visions present themselves, just enjoy the show. Don't worry about what they "mean." Chances are, you're just bouncing around through different images without any real coherency. And when they stop, don't worry about it. They weren't really serving you in the first place, but your ego might miss them and want them to return. Don't let your ego get in your way of being clear!

Engaging with Others

Keep in mind that the more relaxed you become with your ego, the more of a challenge you will become to others who have not relaxed or transcended their egos. Given that egos make it their profession to distort their image in the mirror of reality, the clearer a mirror you become, the more uncomfortable you will make other egos. This is because you will become increasingly less likely to engage in others' ego-dramas, and their egos won't like this. From their perspective, you will be refusing to play the game they want to play the way they want to play it. That will make you something of a party-pooper in an existential sense. Egos don't like that, and they will do everything they can to get you to rejoin the game. It will be your job to be vigilant and responsible with yourself and how you express your energy.

Set and Setting

The environment in which you choose to use entheogens can greatly affect the quality of the subsequent experience. Taking mushrooms at a festival can be fun and novel, but it isn't the best environment for doing serious self-reflective work. Similarly, taking entheogens in a religious context can be a profound way of practicing a religion with others, but the context will probably also provide you with all kinds of illusions, fantasies, and stories to catch your ego's attention and therefore also is not necessarily best for doing genuine self-reflective work. Shamanic contexts likely aren't much better for the reasons listed in the section above about the pluralistic nature of shamanic worldviews. So what is the best set and setting?

Secure and Free From Distractions

First of all, you will want to feel secure in your environment and the people you are with (if anyone). Ideally, you want a location that will not be disturbed by others during the course of your medicine work. If you are at home, this means turning off the phone and the computer and not answering the door if someone comes over. Have a sitter to do that, if necessary. But during the time of your medicine work, you want to be able to stay focused on what you are doing.

Furthermore, your aim is to "go within," so you will want a dark, quiet place in which to do your work. Nighttime is best for a variety of reasons. For one, it will be dark so there will be fewer distractions so you can close your eyes and focus inward. Second, our minds relax more at night. During the day, most peoples' minds are busy thinking about the things they should be doing and should be accomplishing. When you are working with entheogens, you want to be able to focus your mind entirely on the present moment of your experience, not thinking about what you should be accomplishing at that time. It is simply easier for people to enter this relaxed state at night.

To help your mind relax, it is also wise to have all tasks and chores finished for the day before embarking on your inner journey. If something is pressing on your mind, don't leave it until after. Get it done and out of the way so that you don't have to bother worrying or thinking about that issue. This can be especially challenging for people in our modern world where our egos are trained to think that they have to be accomplishing something at every moment and that we should keep ourselves busy and task oriented. Taking up a simple meditation practice can help break this pattern. If you find you are not able to be present when you work with entheogens, then give meditation a try to practice relaxing into the moment.

The Sitter

Many people find having a "sitter" to be comforting when engaging in entheogenic self-exploration. The sitter is not there to be an active participant but rather for support and reassurance, if such should be necessary. The sitter can also take care of any unexpected events, such as visitors.

Beyond comfort and reassurance, sitters can be important for safety as well. Some entheogens produce such radically altered states of consciousness that people may not be aware of their body or body movements. This is especially true with inexperienced users. Until one is familiar with any particular entheogen and how it affects one, it is good advice to have a sitter to make sure that everything proceeds smoothly and no one hurts themselves.

It is also important to keep in mind that one never knows how one will react to working with a new and as-yet-to-be-experienced entheogen. Though rare, some individuals do have health-related reactions and medical attention might become necessary. In such cases, having a sitter can make a crucial difference.

As entheogen users become more experienced, sitters become less necessary. People come to know their own limits and their own reactions. Many find that doing a journey alone is more rewarding than having others present, even if it is just a sitter. But even in such cases, it is good to have a friend who knows what is taking place and will check in with the explorer at an appropriate time after the journey is completed.

Ritual

Many people enjoy adding ceremony and ritual to their use of entheogens. The only reason to incorporate such practices would be personal desire to have ritual. Entheogens are not mysterious, magical substances that require arcane rituals, spells, or incantations. They are perfectly effective all on their own; no ritual required. Yet, ritual can serve to calm nerves, center attention, and create focus. If such is deemed necessary, then ritual can be useful. Ritual can also become an object of attachment and superstition, however, and can unnecessarily obfuscate and muddy the process of working with entheogens. Ritual is just a "container" and has no function or meaning outside of helping to create the set and setting.

Prayer

Prayers are much like ritual: they are great if they help someone get in the right frame of mind, but they can also be an object of attachment. Prayers do not accomplish anything other than helping a person express him or herself and set the tone and feeling for a ceremonial action. Prayers have no actual affect on anything "out there" in terms of either reality or God or spirits. Consider that you are God. So to whom are you praying? Expressing yourself is fine, but don't become attached to having your prayers "answered" or as actually being effective in "calling up spirits" or "energies." You're only talking to yourself.

Setting Intention

Though working with entheogens is largely unpredictable in terms of what kinds of experiences they will open anyone up to at any given time, going into a session with a clear intention can help one to maintain focus through the experience. The most universal intention is simply to remain present and aware, but sometimes having more specific intentions can be useful. For example, if you've become aware of an ego-generated behavior pattern that you'd like to explore and address, set your intention to do so, and repeatedly remind yourself of that intention throughout your session. Though one ultimately does have to surrender to the experience, a great deal of influence can be exerted through repeated expression of intention. This also means cultivating an intention not to be distracted on the journey and consciously bringing one's attention back to the experience and question at hand.

Understanding Your Personal Interface

Despite appearances, you never actually see, feel, hear, taste, or touch anything directly. What we *experience* as reality is actually all a reconstruction within consciousness. In this sense, each individual living being has its own personal virtual reality. Consciousness is a sophisticated mapping mechanism. Through experience, we learn to identify patterns of energy as objects and identifiable phenomena with the data we take in through our senses and process in our consciousness. Raw data comes into our senses and then we apply our internal maps onto that data in order to produce an experience that we can be aware of. For example, if you see something that you are not able to immediately identify, your consciousness will sort through all kinds of possibilities, trying to make a match between internal map and external data. You might have had such an experience while out for a walk on a dark night. You see a shape off in the distance and you start to run through different possibilities as your eyes attempt to discern what it is you are seeing. Is it a person? An animal? A rock? A tree?

Is it dangerous, or friendly? As your mind attempts to process the data, your perception and energetic reaction to the data changes rapidly. Eventually, you're relieved that it's just a rock.

This process works so smoothly and rapidly that most of the time we are completely unaware of how we are actively reconstructing our experience of reality from the raw data of our senses in our consciousness. But experience always works this way: an internal map applied to raw data.

Buddhism proclaims that this process renders all concepts empty of ultimate reality. According to Buddhist teachings, given that our experience of reality is a compilation of relative concepts, they are empty of all ultimate truth and all things are only conventionally true. The only absolute truth is emptiness. For this reason, Buddhists claim that all human thought, philosophy, science, religion, etc. are only conventional truths and have no real ontological reality.

This position is fundamentally wrong for a variety of reasons. The energy that comprises physical, "external," reality and consciousness work according to the same mathematical and geometrical principles. In other words, the underlying energetic matrix of both "inside" and "outside" is fundamentally the same. Simply put, a square in external reality is the same as a square in internal reality because a square is a fundamental geometric shape and the same mathematical principles apply. This is also true of more sophisticated objects. A tree might be a complicated shape with all of its detail, but mathematically, it is a fractal. Our experience of a tree is therefore not a matter of a conventional perception as determined by our concepts: it is a mapping of an internal fractal construct onto the data of an external fractal construct. There is no reason that the mapping can't be one to one, or in other words, a completely accurate representation of energetic reality.

The basic problem with Buddhist philosophy is that it cannot account for mathematics or geometry. While culturally-derived concepts are conventional and relative to culture and perspective, mathematics and geometry are not culturally-derived concepts. Mathematics and geometry are "discovered" and are completely independent of any cultural perspective or lens. Because of this, they are universal. 2+2=4. This is an energetic universal and has nothing to do with cultural concepts or relative truth. It is a fundamental aspect of reality. Mathematics and geometry are the ontological underpinnings of all of reality. As such, they are not "empty."

Consider another example. Music varies from one culture to another; so much so that what is considered music in one culture might be considered noise in another. Musical tastes and styles are always a matter of convention and therefore "empty" of fundamental truth, if we were to ask which style of music is "better," for example. However, music itself is the expression of universal mathematical and energetic principles. What we *think* of music and how we *experience* it might be cultural convention, but rhythm, vibration, harmony, melody, etc. are all mathematical functions. The energetic constructs of music are universal and fundamental expressions of reality.

Working with entheogens is a means to access the more fundamental energetic nature of reality. Consciousness, as mediated through your body, is your personal interface with energy. When one works with entheogens, consciousness and perception are affected so that your interface works in a heightened and amplified fashion. The underlying energetic, mathematical, geometric, and fractal structures of reality become open to direct perception and experience. The stronger the entheogen, the more geometric and fractal one's experience and perception becomes. This is also a major difference between meditation and working with entheogens: meditation tends to simply clear out and empty your personal interface of content (and thus the Buddhist emphasis on emptiness), whereas entheogens open your perception to the underlying energetic constructs of reality. Meditation is largely about calming and clarifying consciousness. Entheogens are a heightened experience of the fundamental nature of reality.

Key Ideas

- Entheogens are tools for self-exploration and learning to be in touch with one's energy
- Working with entheogens can be extremely challenging, so proceeded with caution and self-education
- Avoid attachment to stories that may arise from visionary experiences

- Take ownership of your energy and experience: remember that it is all you
- Set, setting, and context are all important considerations for maximizing the effectiveness of your experience
- Working with entheogens is a method of opening up your personal interface with the divine without any intermediaries: it is direct experience
- Your personal interface works according to the same mathematical and energetic principles as the rest of nature
- Your personal interface is ultimately a sophisticated, interactive mirror

INTERFACING WITH THE DIVINE

The Divine Imagination

Entheogens primarily do one thing: they open up an individual's ability to perceive and experience energy. This takes many forms and can appear as many different kinds of experiences, but all entheogenic experiences are energetic experiences in the same sense that all of reality is made of energy, yet there is still a great deal of diversity.

Working with entheogens is a direct method of accessing the Divine Imagination, the matrix of all possible energetic permutations. The Divine Imagination is accessed directly through your personal interface, or your consciousness as mediated through the structural network of your body. Given that entheogens function as neurotransmitters and that tryptamines are endogenous to the human body, when we add a very small amount of additional tryptamines to our bodies, our interface begins to function in a heightened manner and our ability to perceive and experience energetic forms expands, and with high level tryptamines such as extracted DMT or 5-MeO-DMT, opens completely.

The Divine Imagination is best accessed with eyes closed. In this way, data is no longer being processed from "outside," and instead one can focus consciousness directly on the play of energetic forms of the imagination and consciousness itself. In a very real sense, this is a process of looking into a mirror. Everything that one might experience in such a state is merely a reflection of the self in one form or another. However, given that most people are not prepared to accept themselves as God, these mirror reflections take on all kinds of forms and can appear as an infinite variety of visionary and psychedelic experiences.

Experience in the Divine Imagination has a paradoxical quality to it in that what one experiences is often taken to be "other," or "not self." Keep in mind that human existence is itself paradoxical: you are both an individual living being in a body with a self-identity and God simultaneously. When working in the Divine Imagination, you are actually interacting with yourself as God from your perspective as a unique individual. Until you learn how to recognize yourself in the mirror and accept that it is just you, you will experience the Divine Imagination as *something else*. Rest assured, however, that it is just you.

Archetypal Energies and Fundamental Geometry

One of the most distinctive features of the Divine Imagination is its geometric quality. This is especially obvious during higher-level experiences with tryptamines. Behind closed eyes, intricate kaleidoscopic images undulate and writhe with stunning radial symmetry. Fractals spin their patterns across universal grids. Sophisticated images with distinctive bilateral symmetry shimmer in translucent light of geometric forms. Patterns overlap and interplay with one another. Infinite spectrums of color give form to subtle gradations to energy. The living world of pure energy becomes immediately apparent and open to observation and inspection.

Within these visionary energetic structures we find the fundamental energetic archetypes of manifest reality. Here, in the Divine Imagination, energy exists in potential or archetypal form: that which exists prior to embodiment in physical form. These are not psychological archetypes. They are more energetic blueprints or basic building blocks of reality.

These are the energetic blueprints from which living beings form as well as inorganic physical structures. When observing these energies, it is very easy for the mind to recognize basic energetic forms and begin to structure them into concrete images of creatures, beings, landscapes, etc. When such happens, people tend to describe themselves as having a "vision" or as encountering beings in a visionary realm. These are constructs of the mind, however, and are not actual "encounters" with any other beings, for they are just reflections of yourself.

It is easy to be confused by the Divine Imagination and indeed, it would seem that most of what we take as religious revelation is the product of individuals who have been confused by their experiences within the Divine Imagination. When people have visions, a common claim is that it must have been "real" because it was so far beyond anything that the individual could have imagined that it couldn't possibly be a product of the mind. The problem is that human consciousness is not normally open to such a heightened perception of energetic possibilities and our engagement with our imagination takes place at a very low level of perception. When we work with entheogens, these limiting factors are suspended and our experience of imagination takes on fantastical qualities. Just keep in mind that you are transcending limited, human imagination and entering into the Divine Imagination, where anything and everything is possible.

It is also important to keep in mind that when entering the Divine Imagination, you are opening yourself up to an infinite amount of potential information that will seem to be far beyond anything that you think you personally know or can account for. Remember that you are actually God in human form and God is all things and all living beings. While your vehicle (your consciousness in this body) is not able to process all this information simultaneously, you do have access to it in limited form. This means that there is potentially nothing that you can't know or experience, at least in some sense.

Let's consider an example. In a visionary state, a shaman experiences the spirit of a plant coming to him and telling him how a particular plant can be used to treat some ailment. In the shamanic context, the shaman takes this experience at face value as a communication between two beings. However, this is not what is happening. The shaman is God and is therefore the plant, the shaman, the patient, and the disease. The communication is experienced as something transpiring between beings, but this is a fundamental confusion. Really it is just one being interacting with itself in the illusory form of different characters with different perspectives. In actuality, they are all one. The shaman experiences the knowledge of healing as being granted to him by outside spirits and agencies, but they are really just visionary versions of himself. He is interacting with himself in a mirror. The knowledge he gives himself is something he already knows but just doesn't know that he knows it.

From the Possibilities of the Divine Imagination to the Actuality of Manifestation

Energy is constantly translating from the realm of infinite possibilities into the realm of actuality, or what we collectively call reality. The energetic possibilities in the imagination are what are playing out here in reality, or what is actually taking place. It is important to understand that while there are infinite possibilities in the Divine Imagination, reality itself is unitary. Geometric forms can rapidly morph into beings that change from one form to another very quickly in the Divine Imagination. In reality, such morphing does not take place at an imaginary level but rather takes years of evolution to actually be achieved. Actual reality does not work according to imaginal principles. Reality works according to basic energetic principles that interact and evolve over time to create what is actual. It is possible for the fractal energetic form of a lizard to transform into a human. In the Divine Imagination, this only takes a brief moment. In actuality, it takes millions of years of evolution to be accomplished.

However, human agency plays a direct evolutionary role in this process. While "nature" has to work according to evolutionary principles as structured by mathematical permutations of fundamental energy, there are aspects of the Divine Imagination that humans can recreate freely and manifest as aspects of human culture, which is itself a transcendent feature of biological evolution. Because humans have self-conscious awareness and the physical ability to transform the world around us with our hands, we can choose to move energy to create what we experience in the Divine Imagination. God is therefore no longer limited by physical evolution, but can engage in imaginative, cultural evolution as well.

A great deal of what we identify as human culture is a product of this process, and numerous examples abound. Let's start with art. The earliest expressions of human culture took the form of cave paintings. A near-universal feature of early cave paintings is geometric forms with bilateral and radial symmetry. Lines, grids, and repetition of patterns are common as well. So too are animal-human hybrids and fantastical animals. These are *all* things that humans encounter in the

Divine Imagination in the entheogenic experience. The birth of human cultures therefore coincides with moving energy from the possibilities of the Divine Imagination into physical form through art.

A curious feature of the Divine Imagination is that it is very common for people to perceive patterns of energy that they can immediately identify as being culture-specific. For example, Celtic knots are a common perception with tryptamines. Similarly, people may also encounter what appears to be Meso-American motifs, Islamic arabesques, Buddhist symbols, Aboriginal dot paintings, or Egyptian hieroglyphics. A common, though entirely mistaken, interpretation is that people believe themselves to be having "past life experiences" or "traveling in the astral" to these other times and realms. This is a fundamentally mistaken interpretation, however. What people are experiencing are merely archetypal energy patterns. In other words, there's nothing "Celtic" about seeing a Celtic knot while on tryptamines. The visionary is merely perceiving the same formations of energy that early Celts perceived in their entheogenic trances and then developed as a cultural artistic pattern and aesthetic. The same holds true for other "cultural" motifs in visionary states. These forms of artistic creation and expression all have their source in the Divine Imagination.

Another example is language itself. In the Divine Imagination, all energy is perceived and experienced as being communicative and expressive. All energy has a qualitative and affective aspect to it (think of the expressive quality of music, for example), because all energy is conscious and an aspect of God. Speech and language is the expression of energy with the intent of clear communication. Through entering into the Divine Imagination, humans learned how to make meaning out of energetic expressions and thus the birth of human language.

Even written language seems to have its origins in the Divine Imagination. Ancient societies often claimed that their written language was given to them directly by God. The ancient language of Sanskrit, as a written form, is called *Devanagri,* which means "language of the city of the Gods." It is well known that ancient Indians used entheogens and it is traditionally claimed that Sanskrit was both seen and heard in trance states of consciousness. Thus the written as well as the spoken form of Sanskrit comes directly out of states of heightened perception of energy.

Human architecture also has its origins in the Divine Imagination. Experiences of temples, palaces, pyramids, and other dramatic structures are common in entheogenic visionary states. Inspired by their visions, humans have successfully recreated those visions in actual architecture. It is no coincidence that, traditionally, the grandest examples of human architecture have all been devoted to expressions of religious cultures and traditions. It is also no coincidence that grand religious architecture tends to exhibit significant radial and bilateral symmetry in fractal forms with ratios that reflect the golden mean. These are direct products of the Divine Imagination as actualized through human hands.

Even science and technology has its origins in the Divine Imagination. Though scientists don't often publicize this, many scientific breakthroughs and discoveries were made in dreams and visualizations, and even in some cases with entheogens. Mathematics and geometry were first developed in ancient Greece, India, and Meso-America; all places where entheogens were used as a primary means of religious and cultural activity. Visionary experiences of advanced technology are also common with entheogens. The internet and our basic computer software and hardware systems were mostly designed by entheogen users on the west coast of California. Technology is nothing but the accurate application of knowledge to the energetic structures of reality. Our best technology is immediately inspired by the Divine Imagination.

Clearly religion itself has its origins in the Divine Imagination, but here we largely find a conflation between imagination and reality where the images and experiences in the Divine Imagination are taken literally, rather than as the energetic possibilities that they actually are. The same can be said for modern-day beliefs in UFOs and aliens – imaginal experiences that are taken as literally true.

Overall, it is easy to see that humans, in their most expressive and intelligent forms, are directly inspired by the Divine Imagination.

Infinity Spectrums

Different entheogens provide different forms of access to the Divine Imagination and can be characterized as infinity spectrums. The basic idea here is that while all entheogens potentially open one up to an infinite variety of experiences and perceptions, the spectrums of different medicines are distinct. Let's consider a few examples to understand how this manifests.

Salvia Divinorum

Salvia divinorum is an entheogenic sage plant from Mexico and remains largely legal to possess and use. Salvia is unique in the entheogenic world as its active compound, Salvinorin-A, is not related to any other class of entheogen. Its impact on the nervous system and brain is limited in the sense that it only interacts with one receptor site, as opposed to tryptamines, which interact with a much broader spectrum of receptors.

Experiences with salvia are unique and have an unmistakable quality to them that is easily distinguished from other entheogens. When compared to other entheogens, especially tryptamines, salvia experiences seem *thick, sticky,* and *clownish or cartoonish.* In a very basic sense, the spectrum of salvia experiences is less expansive than tryptamines and as such, by comparison, seem to be comprised of "fewer pixels" and are of a lower or slower vibration.

Take the cartoonish quality of salvia, for example. If salvia is a cartoon experience, then by comparison, DMT is high-resolution computer graphics. The spectrums of colors in salvia experiences are not as varied or as finely detailed as with DMT. Swaths of color are darker, less bright, and tend to be more gross – like the difference between painting with a large brush versus drawing with a fine-tipped pen.

Similarly, the energy of the experience feels thicker and slower than tryptamines. Rather than the buzzing, high-frequency energy of tryptamines, salvia feels like one is getting pushed, pulled, and stretched out like taffy in a taffy machine. It is very common for people to feel pushed over by salvia because of this quality of the energetic experience.

Visually, this often translates into visual images that appear cartoonish or clownish in nature. Many people describe salvia as being like a "funhouse" or "circus," and there is often an odd, ironic sense of humor and absurdity to the experience. Many who go looking for "divine" experiences of angels and heavenly choirs come away from salvia sorely disappointed because all they got was clowns and carnival rides.

At high-level salvia experiences, most people report variations on the same fundamental theme: reality unzips, turns itself inside out a few times, and eventually reassembles back into the familiar. This happens quite rapidly and can be uniquely unnerving, especially as many people forget they've taken salvia when this begins to unfold. Even with eyes wide open, one's immediate environment disappears and all one can perceive is this strange fractal of energy that looks a lot like a hyper-dimensional zipper (and can also appear as conveyor belts, serpents, or "worm holes") that starts to unzip (it really can be uncanny how much this looks like an actual zipper, complete with teeth and all), and as it does, begins to fold over on itself and turn inside out in all directions at once. As it does so, consciousness fractals out, leaving one feeling like there are many "others" present at the same time, and physically one feels the sticky, taffy-like quality of the energy moving through one's body in patterned, fractal form.

Such an experience is a full energetic opening with salvia. One is completely immersed in the energetic state of perception and experience. However, since salvia has a rather limited infinity spectrum, the experience is nearly always the same with the same features and qualities.

Psilocybin Mushrooms

The infinity spectrum opened up by psilocybin mushrooms, which contain forms of DMT, a tryptamine, is far broader than that of salvia. With mushrooms, the energy starts to take on a buzzing quality, as opposed to the slowly oscillating vibrations of salvia. The difference is immediately obvious. What might have appeared as a spectrum of five shades of color with salvia appears as a spectrum of a hundred shades of color with mushrooms. Especially at higher-level experiences, the gradations in color and fine geometry of mushrooms become exquisitely beautiful and captivating and can be a rapturous experience.

Given the fine variations in geometry, it is easier for full visionary experiences to open up with mushrooms than with salvia as there is more structure for your consciousness to work with. Fantastical scenes and creatures are common, especially with eyes closed. Such visions can also seem uniquely realistic and seem to reflect actual reality in a way that salvia often doesn't. Cartoonish and clownish are not common descriptions of mushroom experiences whereas they are for salvia.

Energetically, mushrooms can also make your body vibrate, especially at higher doses. As crystalline structures, DMT molecules amplify your energy, which tends to vibrate your body, especially when there is resistance of any kind (mental, physical, emotional). Relaxing your body can help minimize vibrations as can an internal willingness to let go. They don't hurt, however, and are not anything to worry about, and can actually feel quite good. Relaxing through vibrations tends to bring about deeper experiences, though, so it is usually beneficial not to try and perpetuate vibrations when they occur.

Vibrating is also a clear sign that you are opening to your energy. As your capacity to manage your energy increases, so will the amount of energy that you process. Vibrating helps to break through your resistances and the more open you become, the more blockages you will remove. Sessions with mushrooms can be very useful for this.

Ayahuasca and its Analogues

Ayahuasca is a step up the infinity spectrum scale from psilocybin mushrooms. Ayahuasca is traditionally prepared with DMT containing plants, but is also mixed with 5-MeO-DMT containing plants as well as members of the rather dangerous nightshade family, such as datura or brugmansia.

In terms of sophistication of experience, ayahuasca is very similar to psilocybin mushrooms, but often feels more sophisticated and of a broader infinity spectrum. Vibrations of energy become even more common and stronger with ayahuasca. The feeling of energy moving through one's body and consciousness is even more palpable and immediate with ayahuasca, and the digestive action (purging and diarrhea) accentuates this. Geometric forms and variations of colors and patterns are even more subtle and intricate than with mushrooms, and the experience is more enveloping. It is also quicker acting than mushrooms, so the rise, peak and decline are more dramatic than mushrooms, which also heightens the perception and experience of energy. It takes you further, faster, and in greater beauty and sophistication.

Extracted and Synthetic DMT

Dimethyltryptamine can be extracted from a wide variety of plants, and is even present in high enough quantities in some plants that they can be smoked directly with no extraction and a full DMT experience can ensue. A full DMT experience comes on in about the time it takes to take a breath and lasts for only 10-15 minutes if smoked, or 30-40 minutes if injected (which is a rather uncommon method of consumption of DMT as most vaporize or smoke it). Though DMT is the active ingredient in mushrooms and ayahuasca, in its extracted form it is absorbed and processed must faster than in these other mediums and therefore is far more powerful and intense.

Because of its extremely powerful and fast acting nature, DMT is not necessarily as effective as a "medicine" as are mushrooms and ayahuasca. Mushrooms and ayahuasca give the visionary a good amount of time to explore themselves and receive lessons in the Divine Imagination. DMT, on the other hand, is more of a rocket ride that one really just needs to let happen and remember to breathe. In other words, mushrooms and ayahuasca are much better for people who have "issues" to heal. DMT is best for those who are looking to get comfortable with their fully open energetic state. DMT is therefore a great tool for learning to manage your energy in a highly expanded state.

Body tremors, vibrations, and seemingly involuntary symmetrical movements are common in the wide-open energetic state of a DMT experience. Within the span of a breath, most people find themselves more profoundly altered perceptually and energetically than they ever thought possible as they are flooded with the high-level vibrations of energy that DMT makes accessible. Within this state, reality becomes a hyper-vivid collection of energy patterns, fractals, and geometric kaleidoscopes of radial and bilateral symmetry. These hyper-vivid energy patterns can very easily transform into very real-seeming beings and reports of gods, aliens, alternate realms, and other, strange hybrid beings are very common with DMT experiences. These are all reflections in the mirror of the Divine Imagination, however, and none of them have any ontological reality outside of the immediate perceptual experience.

By comparison, ayahuasca and mushrooms seem like playing in the kiddie pool. A full DMT experience is simply so expansive and total that no amount of work with mushrooms or ayahuasca can really prepare one. At lower levels, DMT is similar to a high-level ayahuasca or mushroom experience, but once a certain threshold is crossed, the range of DMT is just so far beyond these other medicines that comparisons quickly break down. The geometry, fractals, and patterns are always of a family resemblance, however, yet their complexity and sophistication is greater by infinite degrees.

5-MeO-DMT

The crown jewel of all entheogens is 5-methoxy-dimethyltryptamine and can reasonably be called "the God molecule." Infinitely more powerful than DMT, 5-MeO-DMT gives rise to probably the fullest possible energetic expansion that the human body can process. In terms of infinity spectrums, 5-MeO-DMT opens one to the pure infinite nature of all possible energetic permutations. It also fairly effectively dissolves the ego within a few moments if the subject is willing to let go and trust the experience unconditionally. In this sense, for those who are able to let go, an experience of 5-MeO-DMT is a near instantaneous expansion into one's full energetic state as God (within the limits of what can be experienced within the human body). A near-universal reaction by those who have experienced 5-MeO-DMT is that *this experience is definitively IT!* Though it can be challenging to process exactly what that "IT!" is, this conclusion is very difficult to deny. Personally, it was my first experience with 5-MeO-DMT that permanently moved me out of the agnostic/atheist camp into direct knowledge of the existence of God, and in many respects, this entire guide is the product of this transformation and the subsequent understanding of the nature of reality as a unitary, fractal energetic system.

And for anyone who is still inclined to react by saying, "but that's just a drug experience," I will remind you that 5-MeO-DMT is a natural neurotransmitter that is already present in each and every human being on this planet (as is DMT). Given that *all of our experiences of reality are mediated by neurotransmitters, all of reality is a "drug" experience.* With different levels of neurotransmitters in our system, we are able to perceive and experience the energy of reality in different ways. That does not make the perception and experience less real or valid – only different (provided that we can remain clear of confusion through our interactions with the Divine Imagination).

Unlike the other entheogens discussed here, 5-MeO-DMT is largely non-visual in quality. Though it can give rise to perceptions of pure, crystalline fractal rainbow light, visuals are not a defining feature of the 5-MeO-DMT experience (and is a major distinction between 5-MeO and the hyper-visual nature of DMT). Rather, 5-MeO-DMT is more an experience of pure energy beyond any form or representation. And it is quite significant that this energy is immediately perceived to be not only fundamentally true and the actual nature of reality, but it is also experienced as conscious and as being pure, absolute, and unconditional love itself. It is your absolute nature as God, a conscious energy being that is made out of love. 5-MeO-DMT is simply the most pure and clear mirror for experiencing your true energetic nature.

Key Ideas

- Entheogens open one up to experiences of energy in the Divine Imagination
- The fundamental matrix of energy in the Divine Imagination is comprised of patterns and fractal geometry
- Visions in the Divine Imagination arise out of the energetic matrix
- Much of what we take to be cultural products are reflections of energy patterns within the Divine Imagination
- Conscious entry into the Divine Imagination drives cultural evolution and personal expression
- Different medicines open one up to different "infinity spectrums" and therefore have unique characteristics of energy, perception, and experience

The Nature of the Journey

Though each medicine is different, when working with tryptamines, there are some common dynamics of the experience that are worth commenting on. Journeys can be broken down into phases that are fairly consistent. The first phase is onset. With mushrooms this can take up to the first couple hours of the experience. With ayahuasca, the first thirty minutes or so. For DMT the onset is less than 5 minutes. With 5-MeO-DMT it is about 10 minutes. This is the phase where the medicine is building up to its peak, or the most intense and expansive part of the experience. During this onset phase the experience grows in waves. With DMT and 5-MeO, the onset begins with the first breath, but with mushrooms and ayahuasca, it can take up to an hour before the actual onset even begins.

Onset is followed by the peak. This is the most expansive and intense part of the experience. With DMT, and especially 5-MeO-DMT, the peak is so massive and so total that it defies description. It is brief, however, and then the experience begins to return back to baseline. With ayahuasca and mushrooms the peak lasts longer and then there is a gradual return to baseline, with mushrooms taking the longest. It is during the peak that the ego is the most relaxed and people experience their energy in its most expansive state. It is also when most people feel the greatest mystical awareness of themselves as the divine.

To make it successfully through these first two phases, it is important to relax, trust, and let go. Egos can initially react with a great deal of discomfort and distress at the experience of energetically opening up, and these early phases can produce a considerable amount of fear and anxiety. Really, all that can be done is to surrender to the experience, let it unfold as it will, and trust that you will be able to handle it and that you will eventually come back, even though it might not feel like it at the time. Generally, if there is resistance, once it is overcome, it has been dealt with for that particular session and is unlikely to return until sometime after the peak, if at all.

After the peak, the next stage of return then begins to unfold. This is another important transitional moment, for this is when egos start to reassert themselves once more after the initial transcendence through the expansion and peak. At this point, egos start to realize that they are "coming back" and might try and bring the session to a conclusion prematurely. For example, when working with DMT, salvia, or 5-MeO, many people begin to try and vocalize about their experience at this time, commenting on how beautiful, strange, or profound it is. If a sitter is present, this is a good time to remind the person not to rush the experience and continue to focus inwards. The temptation is for egos to bring themselves out of the experience and get back to "normal." However, some of the most important personal revelations can come at this time. The voyager has just been through a radically altered perspective and now has fresh insights to bring to their personal issues and choices. This is a great time to integrate and bring the lessons home and own them. Also, it can be particularly challenging to try and articulate what one has just been through at this time and trying to do so can be distracting from the process that is still at work.

The return is also another phase that can feature significant vibrations. As egos are becoming more present at this time, individuals may begin to feel their resistances and blocks start to reform and this can translate into vibrations in the body, especially of the limbs. This is particularly the case with DMT and 5-MeO-DMT. At this time people may feel that they are unable to manage the high level of energetic vibrations. In extreme cases, this can manifest as purging. More often, however, release is achieved through physically vibrating.

The key to the process of the journey really is the ego. In order for the journey to successfully begin, the ego has to surrender to the process. When egos refuse to surrender, it becomes a "bad trip" as one's God self will happily oblige to work the refusing ego over. Generally, however, egos get the point and relax during the onset phase of the journey. During the peak, the ego is more or less transcended and the voyager is fully enveloped by the experience. As soon as the peak has passed, however, the ego can sense that it is no longer necessary for it to surrender, for the wave have cashed and now the journey back begins. The ego jumps on this opportunity and will attempt to begin reasserting itself immediately. To get the most out of the experience, it is important to remember to continue to surrender and relax the ego. One of the primary ways this can be achieved is through body posture and movement.

Posture and Movement

Though it is popular to describe entheogenic experiences, especially high-level ones, as "out-of-body" experiences, it is important to note that no such thing actually exists or occurs. Keep in mind that while consciousness is not a *product* of the physical body, your perspective as a living vehicle for God is dependent on your body. When one works with entheogens, one is opening up to an energetic experience. By immersing oneself fully in the energetic experience, one enters the Divine Imagination. Here all kinds of experiences and perceptions are possible, and it is very easy for one to forget that one is in a body. Keep in mind that when in the Divine Imagination, one has potential access to any aspect of the divine. Always remember that God is all things and all beings. There is an infinite variety of experiences that await one in the Divine Imagination. All of the energy of the experience is mediated through one's vehicle, however, and energetic experiences are always experiences in the body, which is the locus of your energetic matrix. An "out-of-body" experience, in the literal, as opposed to experiential sense, is an impossibility. (Correlated with this fundamental truth is that there is no such thing as disembodied consciousness or beings – all true beings exist in a body. All experiences of "spirits" or "disembodied beings" are just that – experiences in the Divine Imagination.)

A phrase that is more useful than "out-of-body" is "full energetic opening." When one surrenders and opens fully to one's energy, one is able to energetically experience oneself as not being identified with just the physical body. However, unless one is centered in the core of one's being, a full energetic opening can certainly send one wandering about in the Divine Imagination in such a manner that one has the impression of having left the body behind. However, it is only attention and awareness that has left the body behind. Consciousness itself hasn't actually "gone" anywhere. Reality is *always* a local phenomenon that is mediated through the physical body.

Relax into your center. This is your primary energetic goal when working with entheogens. When the energy opens up, it is easy to get carried away by it. The Divine Imagination turns into a maelstrom of flowing, shifting geometric forms, patterns, and energy. Images arise and stories begin to form. As long as you are not in your center, it will be challenging to recognize all that reveals itself to you as yourself. When you are firmly relaxed into your center, the mirror of self is clear and you can easily recognize yourself in all that you perceive and experience. Maintaining your center in these experiences and throughout your journey is training for maintaining the integrity of your energy in everyday life. Monitoring your body can help tremendously in this process.

Movement and Working with Energy

Give your ego the goal of staying still. This means that you make an agreement with yourself that you will only move when it is absolutely necessary, or if you feel inspired by the medicine to do so. This is a way of keeping your ego in check. Egos want to find ways to distract you from the work that you are doing. Remember that the function of the ego is to maintain the illusion of separation at all costs, and it will use every trick it can think of to pull you back into its sphere of influence. This can translate into fidgeting, physical discomfort, itches, twitches, etc. If you can recognize these distractions and keep your attention focused on the task of exploring your energy, then you can avoid unnecessary movement or adjustments that only serve to bring you out of the moment.

Ironically, the more one relaxes, the more one might feel "moved." This is very different from the physical distractions created by ego. The ego distractions almost always come in the form of "I need to attend to this," "I need to adjust this," "If I can just take care of this, then I'll feel better," etc. Being moved does not have this "personal" quality to it, and in fact, more often feels like one is literally being moved by forces that appear to come from outside oneself. Of course there is nothing outside of oneself, but this is a manifestation of the fundamental paradox of being: You are both a unique individual and God simultaneously. In this sense, your self as God can interact with yourself as "you" in a way that appears as though something exterior is interacting with you. In other words, when working with the medicines, people sometimes feel "possessed" by spirits or energies that seem to compel them to move their bodies or make various sounds.

Though such an experience can be disturbing, it is actually a sign of healthy progress. The key to integrating it successfully and realistically is to own the energy. There is a very serious potential ego trap here. Remember that egos don't want to own the energy. Egos want to convince you that the energy is "other" and will create all kinds of stories and experiences to convince you of this "reality." For example, it is much easier for an ego to convince itself that it was possessed by the "Holy Spirit" that "descended into it" than it is for the ego to accept that you were merely experiencing yourself. Similarly, it is easier for an ego to accept that it was possessed by a demon rather than own up to the fact that all that negative energy is the result of the individual playing too many ego games that have prevented the individual from properly and honestly expressing itself. To truly integrate yourself and your experience and reside in your energetic center, you have to own all of this energy – the "good" and the "bad." It is *all you*, so own it. Don't put the responsibility off on someone or something else, even God. It's *all you!*

The more you own the energy and take responsibility for it, the closer you will get to your energetic center (which is also the center of *all things and the "location" where God resides)*. Physically, this is the center of your heart, which is also from where the strongest electromagnetic field of your physical body emanates in the form of a torus (another torus of electromagnetic energy is produced by the brain, but it is far weaker than the torus of the heart). To get to the center of your heart, there could be a great deal of energy you need to work through. If you have lived a life of suffering, pain, judgment, fear, anxiety, frustration, dissatisfaction, etc., then chances are you've built up all kinds of personally harmful patterns of behavior, choice, and reaction. You'll need to unwind all of these patterns and energetic residues in order to successfully relax in the center of your heart and being. Given that most people have these patterns, most people have some work to do to discover and own their true center.

Coming to own your energy is like doing a dance or playing a game with yourself. When you begin, your energy can definitively feel like something outside and exterior to you, as does the deepened level of consciousness that comes with it. The more you work with it, the more your sense of personal identity can expand outside the usual confines of your ego. As you do this, the "distance" between "you" and the energy you perceive and experience as coming from outside of you collapses. When you eventually reach the center of your being, the difference is completely obliterated and you are able to take responsibility and ownership for all of your energy, not just the energy that your ego tries to convince you is "you."

Perceptually, one's "visions" will change as this process progresses. The more you own your energy, the more likely you are to see fractals, geometry, and energy patterns as opposed to visions of beings, creatures, landscapes, and other specific imagery. Remember that all "visions" arise out of a fundamental matrix of fractal geometry. The more you can stay focused on the energetic matrix, the less prone you are to being caught by ego-generated illusions. Visually, the geometry tends to exhibit more coherency and symmetry when you are in a centered state. This is a more accurate reflection of yourself in the mirror of the Divine Imagination than any "vision" that contains specific imagistic content. God, after all, is not any *thing*. It is the energy from which all *things* arise, and that energy functions according to the parameters of fractal geometry. When you are able to perceive yourself clearly, this is what you will see.

The perfect symmetry of the centered state is also reflected in body movements and posture in that centered individuals tend to exhibit mirrored bilateral symmetry in their physical movements (when letting themselves be moved by the energy without resistance). Movements also take on a flowing character, usually after one has processed through their resistance in the form of vibrating or convulsing. Once the body has been accustomed to the energy and resistance has broken down, then the vibrations can manifest as smooth, fluid, mirrored, symmetrical movements. This can only occur when the ego is suspended or transcended. Vibrations indicate that the ego is still struggling with the energy. Smooth movements indicate that the struggle has been released.

Maintaining Posture

How you hold your body has a direct and immediate impact on your entheogenic experience and should always be kept in mind in order to maximize the effectiveness of any entheogenic session. Consider the following guidelines:

Uncrossed appendages

Keep arms and legs uncrossed at all times. This is simple energetics and there is no deep metaphysical secret here. Your central core of energy is found along your central axis and runs from your head to the base of your torso. It is along this axis that your central energy centers are located in your physical being. Your arms and legs are then conduits and energy channels, but not energy centers. Always keep in mind that your bio-physical energy is electromagnetic and therefore carries a positive and negative charge. When you cross your arms or legs, you are actually crossing over energy currents. There isn't anything necessarily "wrong" with this, other than that it can make the energy of the experience more convoluted, like crossing over two wires that really shouldn't be touching. You'll have a far easier time remaining centered in your natural flow if you keep your arms and legs uncrossed. Remember: your energy is perfectly symmetrical in a bilateral fractal expression. Crossing arms and legs perturbs your natural bilateral symmetrical expression. It can also create muscle cramps and physical discomfort due to the confused energy flow. This is easy to avoid: just remain uncrossed and symmetrical.

Sitting

When working with medicines in a seated position, your main concern is to keep the above issue of uncrossed appendages in mind in order to maximize your smooth energy flow. This means if you are seated in a chair, keep both feet planted firmly on the floor, ideally keeping your feet flat. Energy grounds out through your feet and keeping your feet flat allows for a smoother transfer of energy, as opposed to being on tip toes, for example. Keep in mind that large energy discharges can create "energy burns" on your toenails. It doesn't hurt (though it might prick and tingle), but it can make toenails look pretty ugly. Keeping your feet flat can help minimize the possibility of this happening. If it does, don't worry – your toenails will eventually grow out and look pretty again!

Also, when seated in a chair, keep your back straight and your arms at your side. It is best to keep you hands on your lap with palms facing up. Remember that body posture communicates receptivity at an energetic level. Having your palms facing up energetically says, "I'm ready to receive." Putting your hands down says, "I'm keeping to myself." Also, putting your hands on your legs can cause energy to flow from your hands into your legs and can make discharging and grounding through your feet more of an issue than it might otherwise be. Always keep in mind that your hands are powerful conduits and are extremely sensitive to energy.

When sitting on the floor, many people want to sit in a meditation position (lotus, half-lotus or crossed legs) as this is what they are accustomed to through their mediation practice. Meditation is about calming the mind and transcending the concerns of the body, however, whereas medicine work is about opening to energy. While meditation and medicine work have some similarities in practice, they are actually quite different modalities of work, and thus the postures of one modality don't necessarily translate into the other. For medicine work, crossed legs are not recommended for the energetic reasons listed above. Thus, when sitting on the floor, legs should be kept out straight or legs can be bent with the soles of the feet pressed together. This last posture makes for a nice, contained energy circuit. Your legs will make a diamond shape in front of you. This provides a nice base to sit on and does not confuse the energy at all.

When sitting in this manner, you might be tempted to hold your feet with your hands. There is nothing wrong with this, but be aware that you can created an intense energy loop by doing so and can build up a significant charge in your body. This can manifest as serious muscle cramping and a feeling of overheating in your core. If this occurs, crouch down and place your feet and hands flat on the ground and take some deep breaths, letting your breath pass out of you slowly. This will help to ground out the energy. As soon as you feel better, resume your position and continue your journey.

As with sitting in a chair, when sitting on the floor, be mindful of your hand positions. The best position, and most reflective of openly receiving, is keeping hands at your sides or lap, palms up, ready to receive. This is passive reception, however, and not grasping or desiring. It is a body posture that says, "I'm not necessarily looking for anything in particular, but am ready and willing to receive whatever comes my way, regardless of what I think about it." This is a body posture that helps put the ego in its place.

While it is your goal to avoid fidgeting, be mindful of how the energy is moving you. If you feel the energy moving your hands or arms, set your ego aside and let it happen. You may find that your hands spontaneously start forming into what Buddhists and Hindus call mudras (think of statues of Buddhas and Hindu deities and their hand gestures). It might be tempting to think that such a phenomenon *means something*. Don't give into the temptation. It does *not* mean that you are a bodhisattva or an avatar or anything else! All it means is that you are being willing and open to letting the energy move you.

Another spontaneous hand gesture is the "prayer" gesture of hands open and pressed together before the heart. If you feel you need to center yourself, this is a good gesture to make. When you feel centered, return your hands to the neutral position on your lap. Don't be surprised when, as you naturally become more centered, your hands seem to float into this position all of their own accord as you open to the energy flowing through you. This is a good sign, but don't get attached to it!

The more relaxed you become and the closer you get into your center, the more likely you are to spontaneously move in mirrored symmetry with your arms, and making the "prayer" gesture is just the beginning. Energy is always flowing by its very nature and is never static. In terms of body movements, this means that your arms will start to move in flowing, fluid movements the more centered you are in the energy. When you are truly centered, all of your movements will exhibit total mirrored bilateral symmetry. In other words, your hands and arms will mirror each other and will function together as a unit. However, your arms will not cross over each other and at most your hands will come together and meet in the middle to mirror each other. When energy is working naturally and spontaneously, energy currents do not cross over one another: they mirror each other.

Lying Down

The same conditions that apply to sitting apply to lying down. Arms should be kept at your sides with palms open, facing upwards. Legs should be kept uncrossed and slightly spread apart. Don't move unless you feel inspired to do so.

The temptation, when lying down and things become difficult or challenging, is to move from a relaxed and open position to a closed and protective position. Generally, this takes the form of the fetal position. People curl up and try to energetically close themselves off from the experience. Given that it is impossible to close yourself off from the energy once you've taken a medicine, resorting to the fetal position is a means of trying to ride out the experience in a protective state. Chances are, this will make for a bad trip. Though it can seem frightening, bring yourself back to an open and receptive position whenever this happens.

Another common form of resistance takes the form of rolling from side to side or repeatedly turning over in place. This happens when people resist letting the energy flow in symmetrical movements. The rolling allows the energy to move, but it is in a confused and "unnatural" way as the movements are a product of resistance. If you are able, once more bring yourself back to a symmetrical posture and hold your body in a state of openness, rather than resistance.

Fractal Energetic Yoga

Though I am currently the only person that I know of who can do this, what you are eventually headed for is the ability to perform what I call fractal energetic yoga. Once you have cleared away all of your resistance and fully taken ownership and responsibility for your energy, you should be able to perform fractal energetic yoga. I perform these exercises on a daily basis, and when I work with the medicines as well. As a regular exercise, I find that they help keep me centered and authentic with my energy.

To begin, I sit on the floor with the soles of my feet and palms of my hands pressed together. I then begin flowing with the energy by rolling onto my back. Using a minimum of muscle and a maximum of energy, I then lift my legs into the air, with my arms making fluid motions at my sides and my heels pressed together. When I do so, I am able to balance on a single point on my spine and do not need to use my muscles to hold myself up. In other words, this is something of an energetic balancing exercise through the authentic use of bio-physical energy. I then go through free-form series of fluid movements using all of my body as a mirrored symmetrical energetic system. It's fantastic exercise and is a genuine expression of my innate fractal geometry and energy.

The more centered you become in your energy, the more you should be able to do such exercises and the more natural and normal they should feel. Don't hurt yourself, but try experimenting! You can do this with or without the medicines. (A video sample of Fractal Energetic Yoga is available for viewing on my webpage, www.martinball.net)

Voicing

Another key area where energy is expressed is through voicing and vocalizing. As with body movement, the same fundamental distinction applies in terms of making an agreement with yourself not to speak or say anything unless you feel inspired to do so. This is a method for learning how to distinguish between the expressive impulses of your ego and the expressive impulses of your genuine energy.

Voicing and expressing energy linguistically can take different forms for different people. A common experience is to "speak in tongues." Such an experience has no "religious" meaning whatsoever and is not a "sign" of anything, other than that the person exhibiting this behavior is letting themselves express their genuine energy. In this sense, glossolalia can be understood as pure "energy language." It is a direct translation from one form of energy into another without any specific meaning or linguistic intent.

Others experience vocal energetic expression in the form of "mediumship" or "channeling." With such behaviors, people generally feel that their consciousness is being inhabited by some kind of being or intelligence that exists outside of it and wants to express itself through the vehicle of the person having the experience. Many religions and spiritual traditions promote such kinds of experiences as valid contact with "spirits," "ancestors," "ascended masters," and other such related interpretations. These "channeled" beings and voices are merely part of the subject's consciousness, however, and no matter how "other" they seem, this is only an ego projection. When a person takes ownership of their energy, this projected distinction dissolves.

In cases of unresolved energy, "mediumship" experiences can become more like possession experiences. These are extreme cases where people are not owning their energy and taking responsibility for themselves. Voices, body posture, and movements can all alter radically, giving the strong impression that "something" has taken someone over. These are all just ways that energy expresses itself, however, and should not be taken to be a literal possession in any sense. If a person can take ownership of their energy, the "possession" will dissolve in an instant.

Though it can feel silly to one's ego, a perfectly effective method for dealing with vocal phenomena is to have conversations with yourself. If you find that you start to manifest strange voices that seem to compel you to speak when you work with the medicines, take the opportunity to speak with the voices. It is actually quite easy to get into a conversation with yourself in this manner and you might be surprised at how easily your voice switches between what you would normally identify as "your" voice and the voice of the "being" inside you. The two voices can sound completely unlike each other. They are both you, however, and this should be understood as a game or as role-playing. Just like in a dream, the character of "you" can interact with other characters that you experience as "not you," but they are you, just the same. Taking responsibility for your energy means learning how to own those expressions of energy that seem to be "not you." Vocalizing and speaking in different voices is just one of several mediums through which to practice this.

Speaking in voices and feeling inspired to say things is not the same as hearing voices in your head. Some people hear voices when they work with medicines or enter into altered states of consciousness. In general, my advice is not to listen to the voices. Voices heard in the head are projections of the ego. They are not genuine expressions of innate energy. For example, when considering what to do in ordinary life, you may hear a voice in your mind giving you advice in considering your question. That voice can easily lead you astray by playing off of your ego. Rather, when considering what choices to make, center your attention on what you feel, not the voices in your mind. This will *always* give you a clearer reading on the actual state of your energy. The same holds true for working with the medicines. Don't pay attention to the voices in your head, but rather focus on what you feel. Remember that it is the role of the ego to convince you of the reality of its illusions at all times, and one of its primary methods to do so is through internal dialogue and projection.

Purging

Occasionally, energy needs to be released through purging. Some medicines, such as peyote and ayahuasca, lend themselves to such experiences more than others. However, virtually any medicine can lead to purging, depending on what is happening at a personal, energetic level.

In traditional shamanic cultures, purging is generally understood to be a cleansing and purifying act to remove negative energy from a person. This is not necessarily the case. Purging tends to occur when people resist the energy of their experience, in one way or another. Even the most cosmic sense of needing to purge or vomit can be turned around in an instant if resistance can be let go of. If one is not able to let go of the resistance, then the medicine could force it out of the individual through purging. It is not necessary to go through a purge, however, in many cases. For example, though ayahuasca makes many people purge, some people rarely, if ever, purge with this medicine.

Purging also occasionally occurs with DMT and 5-MeO-DMT. With these medicines, purging is most likely at the very beginning of the experience where the ego may still be trying to resist and hold on, or at the transition between the peak and the return to baseline. After the peak, the ego gets the idea that it can eventually regain control, so it starts to reassert itself after the temporary suspension during the peak. At this time, your ego may try and convince you that "this is too big," or "this is too much energy" and "you can't handle this." Your body may then react by purging or vomiting.

Many people start to release energy before working with medicines as well, due to anxiety and anticipation, especially before working with such overwhelmingly powerful medicines as DMT and 5-MeO. Here people may find that they need to use the restroom several times before beginning their journey. Defecation and urination are both ways of releasing pent up energy and freeing yourself up energetically. Others may find that they suddenly have a great deal of gas and they need to burp or break wind. If any of these things happen to you, don't judge yourself and just give yourself the time and space to let the energy work itself out. There's nothing to be embarrassed or self-conscious about.

Key Ideas

- Ego responses determine the quality of an entheogenic journey
- Ego resistance produces difficult journeys
- Egos will begin to reassert themselves immediately after the peak of the experience
- Remember to relax and let go
- Body posture can significantly affect your experience
- Be mindful of your body
- Avoid distracting yourself with unnecessary movement or sound
- Let the energy of the experience move you, not your ego
- Let the energy of the experience inspire your voice and choice of words, not your ego
- Working with entheogens is a method of practicing letting your natural energy express itself without the constraints of the ego

Trust

Ultimately, working with entheogenic medicines is about coming to know yourself and your energy. Though entheogenic experiences can be frightening and intimately challenging, it is important to rest in a state of trust. You can trust that transcending your ego is the only genuine path to liberation and true personal happiness, and that whatever work you require yourself to go through in order to attain this is worth it. In the end, there is no difference between trusting God and trusting yourself, for you are, after all, one and the same. You can rest assured that whatever "God" puts you through on your journey to claiming personal responsibility is exactly what "you" need.

Entheogenic experience is a heightened experience of energy and therefore is a heightened experience of your life. All of your "issues" become amplified and exaggerated in the entheogenic experience so that you may become aware of their true nature, and how you are personally exercising choice and free will to create your reality. While a great deal of reality is a given, there is a tremendous amount of room for us to express free will and choice, and nowhere is this more apparent than in how we choose to take responsibility for our energy and for our reactions. Shit happens. We can't control that. However, we can control how we choose to react when shit happens, and this is how we master our energy and take responsibility for it. You, as God, are *never a victim.* Only egos are victims.

Working with entheogens is about learning how you are actively creating illusions and ego dramas in your life through the failure to take responsibility for yourself, your energy, and the games that you create through your ego. Diving into the energetic world is diving into the patterns that make up your life. It is a process of looking into the mirror of who and what you are in order to get clear on precisely how you are choosing to create your experience. This is not easy work. It is *much* easier for egos to blame others for their problems or look to outside sources for resolution – indeed, virtually all religions and political and social systems play off this weakness of the ego. Liberating yourself from your ego means not only liberating yourself from yourself, but also from religion and social manipulations as well. This is a process of developing true freedom. But true freedom comes with complete personal responsibility. Freedom and responsibility are two sides of the same coin, and one cannot be achieved without the other.

Working Through Your Lessons

Everything that you experience at every moment holds a potential reflective lesson for you. All of reality is a mirror – no exceptions! I guarantee you that *you have lessons to learn and issues to work on.* Transcending the ego does not make your lessons and issues disappear. In fact, in most instances, the ego is transcended for only a brief period of time, such as when actively engaged with the medicines, but then quickly reasserts itself as soon as it is able. Working with medicines is therefore a practice. It is about learning what it feels like to transcend your ego and take responsibility for yourself while resting in the trust of your innate energy. This is easy to do when 5-MeO-DMT blows your ego out of the water, but it is much harder to maintain during everyday experiences when our egos are confronted by illusions, dramas, and fantasies on all sides by every single person we meet. Maintaining a state of transcendence and liberation from the ego takes constant attention, honesty, integrity, and willingness to trust your energy, even when it makes you or others uncomfortable (people who have transcended their egos tend to make those who are trapped in their egos uncomfortable for the basic reason that egos habitually live in illusion and do not like to have their illusions challenged).

It is therefore important to understand that the ability to maintain a state of ego transcendence is not the product of a single experience of transcendence, or even many. In other words, merely working with entheogens won't accomplish this goal in-and-of-itself. Plenty of people have worked with entheogens for millennia but are still caught in all kinds of ego-generated illusions. To return to an earlier example, Terence McKenna explored all kinds of entheogens but still got thoroughly entrapped by his projections of UFOs, aliens, and machine elves. By the analysis presented in this guide, he completely failed to recognize himself in the mirror and instead got drawn in by fantasy and projection. Entheogens are by no means a "magic bullet."

Entheogens do produce relatively reliable instances of transcending the ego, or at least setting it aside temporarily as fear and self-protection are suspended for the duration of the onset and peak of an entheogenic experience. This is simply practice, however, and a medium for becoming familiar with the experience, and with the nature of one's energy. People must actively choose to remain in trust and suspension of the ego through constant attention to their energy and their choices in all moments. The task of staying present with your energy is a constant requirement of perpetuating and achieving your personal liberation. Commit yourself to trust and honesty and you can do it for yourself, but remember that you are the only one who can do it. No one else can ever do it for you. It's 100% up to you.

When you work consciously with the medicines, what you will find is that you will move through various stages of lessons and experiences. Even though different medicines give rise to different kinds of experiences, remember that all uses of entheogens are an entry into your own mind and energy. You, as God, know everything about yourself and know everything that you need to face as an individual to get clear on how you are responsible for your reality. You cannot hide from what you already know about yourself!

Many people who work with medicines comment on how the medicine seems to know everything about them – even things they didn't remember actively. The medicines seem to know exactly what to show you and what kind of experience to bring to you and when. It is as though you have entered a schooling program built with interactive media that is designed perfectly just for you. It is simply astounding how *personal* and *intimate* the experience can be. This is only surprising if you think that it is merely a "drug" experience, or if you think that the medicine has some mysterious spirit in it that somehow knows everything about you. When you understand that you are God and that the medicines allow you to look at yourself in the mirror of the Divine Imagination, then none of this should be surprising in any way. In fact, *it is precisely what one would expect to find and it works exactly as one would expect it to.* Working with the medicines is simply an entry into your personal interface with yourself as God. There's nothing mysterious, magical, or supernatural about it. It is just the way that it works!

Through their lessons, what entheogens reveal is that our authentic energy is just beneath the surface of our egos. Lessons into our true energy are present and with us all the time and it is the ego that attempts to obscure this. This energy is always present and always looking to express itself authentically. God is not something distant, far away, or other. God is within you, *is you*, right here, right now, in all moments. Transcending your ego is merely about relaxing the hold your ego has on you and living authentically in the reality that you are a vehicle for the expression of God's innate energy. Though such a realization changes everything, it really isn't such a big change, given that *you already are God.* It is not about developing new abilities or becoming some kind of spiritual super-human. You already are everything that you will ever be and you already have all the talents and abilities you will ever express. In other words, being awakened to being God in a body is *identical to being fully human by taking complete responsibility for yourself.*

The thought of taking responsibility can seem overwhelming. Egos don't like to take responsibility. They'd rather dish out blame, claim rewards, and indulge in illusion. Many people expend a great deal of energy simply avoiding as much responsibility for themselves as possible, especially religious fundamentalists and dogmatic politicos. The idea of taking responsibility seems daunting, challenging, and ultimately, not much fun (for some reason, egos seem to equate fun with release from responsibility). Though it may seem this way, actually, the opposite is true.

For one, being responsible is not about being responsible for all things all at once. Rather, it means taking responsibility for your energy and expression in each moment. In each moment, there is only a limited amount of energy present that anyone needs to attend to. For example, when you think about your responsibilities in your life, if you consider them all at once, it can seem like a lot. However, the reality is that in each moment, there are only certain things that need to be addressed and dealt with authentically. To be responsible for all things, all you need to do is be responsible with what is before you right now. It's like the saying, "a thousand mile journey begins with one step." When in the moment, all you're actually concerned about is taking one step. Then one more. Then one more. Then one more. Eventually, you will have walked a thousand miles. Or consider writing a book. Taking on the task of writing a book is a big responsibility and commitment. However, every book is written one word at a time, and that's where you put your focus. Stay present in the moment and before you know it, you'll have accomplished your task! If you are confused about what to pay attention to in the moment, go back to the medicines. Through them, you'll show yourself what you need to pay more attention to. Receive your lesson, apply it to your daily life, and stay focused and committed to your path of authenticity and personal responsibility.

The Fruits of the Work

The ironic truth of being human is that, aside from the challenges of being a physical being in a physical reality where shit happens (earthquakes, floods, disease, famine, physical accidents, etc.), the vast majority of problems that humans suffer from are caused by humans themselves. Through technology and science we can gain some limited mastery over the effects of natural disasters and physical and biological problems. As physical beings, protecting our bodies, our vehicles, is a natural and necessary activity. Fear of physical suffering and avoidance and prevention of pain are reasonable, rational measures for us to take.

Yet humans cause far more trouble for themselves than nature. Has there ever been a period in human history when we have not fought each other? Have religions actually brought peace and happiness, or do they fill people with fear, judgment, self-righteousness and self-loathing that then leads to discrimination, genocide, slavery, and war? Have any political systems actually brought about an end to human suffering and created equality for all? Have our economic systems brought happiness and satisfaction, or do they promote exploitation, manipulation, and the fabrication of needs, goods, and services for the gratification of the ego? Is there any culture on Earth where people are truly free? Do any cultural, political, or religious systems actually teach people to take responsibility for themselves and their happiness and authenticity, or do they instead create divides between "us" and "them," "self" and "other," "good" and "bad," "right" and "wrong" and avoid responsibility in the process? Do societies encourage people to be themselves, or some socially-determined and ego-manipulated version of how people "should be" or "should" express themselves?

Nature and the basic facts of physical reality come with being human. There will be suffering and there will be physical pain. Shit will happen. However, *none* of the problems caused by humans or human societies, religions, cultures, and political systems are necessary. *All* of these problems are the product of confused and illusion-bound egos. Therefore *all* of these problems *have the potential to be transcended.* Just imagine if every single person on this planet took responsibility for him or herself to get clear on their authentic energy. No more ego games or dramas. No more fear, judgment, or manipulation. No more illusions propped up by religious and cultural institutions. Though it would take a collective effort to reorganize how society actually functions, the foundation for the vast majority of causes of human suffering could vanish in a very short period of time. In other words, if everyone could take responsibility and actually live in reality and not ego-generated illusion, this would be a profoundly transformed world. It would be a world of radical freedom, and radical responsibility. It would be a completely different world from the one we collectively inhabit now. It would be a world of peace and happiness *for all.*

Key Ideas

- Trust in yourself and your experience
- Be willing to surrender to whatever arises
- Everything you encounter is a mirror reflection
- You will present lessons to yourself
- These lessons are always relevant to your everyday life, choices, and actions
- By becoming aware of your choices, you can learn how to choose differently to better serve your higher good
- Taking ownership of your experience brings you closer to your center and to actual reality
- You always have free will: how you choose to express your energy and live your life is completely your choice
- Being authentic leads to increased self-responsibility, and ultimately, radical liberation from all illusion
- Liberation is the key to peace and happiness for all

RESPONSIBILITY

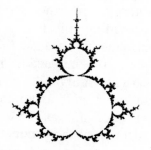

Taking Responsibility

It all begins with you. No one can sort out your ego for you, or the ways you make yourself suffer at the hands of your ego. No one can express your authentic energy for you. *You are the only one who can help yourself.* Others can inspire you and give you good advice and maybe even provide you with a good model for your own choices and actions, but *you have to do the work for yourself.*

A corollary to the above is, if you want to make the world a better place and help others, attend to yourself. You can achieve a lot of "good" in the world and help alleviate suffering through social action, politics, and the "good works" of religious activities, but none of these are real solutions. Your ego may react by saying this is narcissistic or egotistical, but this is just your ego talking – feel free to ignore it! *The only authentic path to helping the world is by helping to free yourself from the illusions and limitations you have placed on yourself through participation in ego-generated illusions and fantasies.* Everything else is just an ego game.

Authentic action is self-motivated action. For example, I am writing this guide, which I sincerely hope will help you and potentially change the world in profound and beautiful ways, but I am not motivated by the thought of actually helping you. *You are not my responsibility.* Your choices are your own, as is your life. What you choose and what you do with your life *is completely up to you and makes no real difference to me.* I am not, then, actually trying to help you in any way or make your life any better. You are your own problem, not mine.

However, for me to be authentic and true to my energy, I simply *must write this guide.* Anything less would be being untrue to myself and my own personal energy. In other words, my motivation for writing this guide and providing this true account of the nature of reality and human experience is because this is important to me, personally. I care about the truth, and because I am committed to being authentic with myself, I care about expressing the truth. Because I care about others (and because I also understand and accept that we are all one being), I care whether others are able to live in truth and reality or not. I care that people suffer from the products of their own egos and illusions. Because I care, not acting on that would be inauthentic of me. I would not be being true to myself. *My primary concern is to be true to myself.* It's the only thing that I can truly take any responsibility for, and I care about doing my part to take responsibility. My motivation is 100% self-motivation. And keep in mind that since we are, in reality, all the same being, being true and authentic with yourself will naturally be of benefit to others, though it will be up to them to take responsibility to realize those benefits for themselves.

Responsibility for Evolutionary Integrity

While humans are neither personally nor collectively responsible for evolution itself, given that our actions have such a dramatic impact on the ecology of the planet, we are collectively and individually responsible for the *evolutionary integrity* of the biosphere. As an individual human, it is reasonable to take actions and precautions to protect your vehicle. After all, you can't lead much of a life if your body is severely physically damaged or compromised. The same holds true, at another scale, for evolution itself. God is all living beings collectively and simultaneously. It was *all* of evolution that brought us to the point where we are now. Since we are God, too, then we are also all of evolution. Therefore, protecting the integrity of the evolutionary system is on par with protecting the physical integrity of our personal vehicles. Evolution is a collective process and we are products of that process. Protecting evolutionary integrity is therefore ultimately protecting ourselves. It is part of our responsibility to be true and authentic to ourselves.

Currently, given the state of the world and its patterns of economic development, environmental destruction, and pollution, we are doing an extraordinarily poor job of protecting the integrity of the evolutionary system. Countless numbers of species have already been lost as a direct result of our disruptive actions at rates that far surpass anything that might occur naturally. And, with our technology, we have the stunning capacity to virtually wipe out all life on this planet in the blink of an eye. We have collectively reached a potentially disastrous point in time. To put it very bluntly, we could really fuck up this little project called life that God has been busy working on for the past few billion years. To put a new spin on an old theological question: Can God create itself as a physical being with so much capacity to affect reality that it could potentially ruin the evolutionary project? Apparently, the answer is yes. We are living proof, as is the world we currently live in.

Through our collective choices and actions, we have made the integrity of the evolutionary system our responsibility. With the development of science and technology, coupled with ego-generated illusions and fantasies, this was perhaps inevitable. Now that the effects of our choices and actions are obvious, the only responsible thing to do is to actively take responsibility. This is ultimately no different from taking personal responsibility. Evolution is the natural expression of energy as expressed through living beings in physical form. Being authentic with ourselves means allowing our natural energy to express itself and being true to that. Being true and authentic with evolution means letting the system run its course, naturally. Just as ego games interfere with our personal expression of our energy, so too do human activities interfere with the expression of evolutionary energy by radically altering environments, polluting them, and causing the widespread extinction of species. We are creating unforeseen consequences for ourselves and for all living beings on this planet. As conscious embodiments of God, it's time to take responsibility. No one and no thing will do it for us. It's up to us.

Children and Responsibility

Children present a special case of personal responsibility. Most parents see it as their job to shape and mold their child into a "good person" and a "good citizen," and also maybe a "good" member of a particular religion. Ultimately, these are misguided goals and are locked into ego-projections of what is "good."

As a parent, you have two primary jobs in relation to your child. This first is to care for it and protect it physically, as it is not able to assume this responsibility itself. It is a child, after all, and needs the care and protection of adults in order to insure its safety and well-being.

Your second job as a parent is to do everything you can to support your child in discovering, owning, and being itself. This *does not mean that you actively mold the child to come out the way you personally want*. Who and what your child is in terms of his or her own personality may have nothing to do with how you think he or she should be. Your job is to provide the context and environment that will allow the child to discover him or herself for him or herself, and, if you are able, present a responsible model for the child.

Other than these two things, parents do not really have any other valid responsibilities toward their children. When children grow up and mature, they become responsible for themselves, just like everyone else, and then it is no longer the parents' responsibility to physically care for the child or provide a context for the child to be him or herself. Upon maturity, these responsibilities then shift to the young adult.

Realistically, most parents expend a great deal of energy trying to make their children be what the parents want them to be. Our societies are even built on such an expectation. Virtually all religions, educational systems, and cultures promote shaping children into pre-determined expectations of who and what they should be and how they should behave or act. Children are not encouraged to be themselves and are not given adequate context or guidance for exploring their own self-natures and energy. In turn, children learn how not to take responsibility for themselves and are indoctrinated into ego-projected fantasies and illusions, often forcefully at the hands of parents, clergy, and educators. Is it any wonder that people in the modern world have such a challenging time getting to know themselves or taking responsibility for their energy? Virtually *everything* is working against them, including their parents, those who could play the greatest role in helping them to be themselves and take responsibility for their lives.

Being Yourself

In the end, it all comes down to being yourself and taking responsibility for who and what you are. There is no grand destiny or purpose waiting for you to discover. You came into this world with free will, and so shall it always be. What you do with yourself and your life is always and forever your choice. Looking for purpose or answers outside of yourself is a distraction from who and what you truly are. You have the ability to liberate yourself and take responsibility for your life. You have the ability to claim your own peace, happiness, and fulfillment. You have the capacity to do the personal work that will help bring about world peace and universal liberation. The energy is inside you and the tools to help you see yourself clearly in the mirror, the entheogens, are there to help you and guide you along your path. Everything you need is right here, right now.

So what are you waiting for?

Step up and take responsibility. Be yourself. Be free.

Be the Divine Being that YOU ARE!

It is the greatest thing you could ever do for yourself or anyone else.

Be bold, take chances, be yourself, and most of all, have fun!

Welcome, at long last, to reality.

Entheogenic Affirmations

      I'd like to end with a few entheogenic affirmations to help remind you to keep it real. They're meant to be fun and a little whimsical. "Spirituality" is so often presented with such earnestness that the absurdity of reality gets overlooked. Egos take everything so seriously! Life is serious, but it's also the most ridiculous game ever, and a great deal of fun, too. So whenever your ego steps and in starts getting all dramatic and serious on you, give it a little reminder with one of these entheogenic affirmations, or ones of your own creation.

      Guess what? You are God! Now get over it =)

      You are God's altered state!

      God doesn't take you seriously, so why should you?

      Your sense of humor is Divine!

      Mirrors mirrors, everywhere . . . Enjoy the Funhouse!

      Everything is an Illusion . . . Except Reality!

      If you won't be your True Self, then who will?

OTHER BOOKS BY MARTIN W. BALL, PH.D.

Available at www.martinball.net and on-line retailers

- *Mushroom Wisdom: How Shamans Cultivate Spiritual Consciousness* (Ronin Publishing, 2006)

- *Sage Spirit: Salvia Divinorum and the Entheogenic Experience* (Kyandara Publishing, 2007)

- *The Entheogenic Evolution: Psychedelics, Consciousness and Awakening the Human Spirit* (Kyandara Publishing, 2008)

- *Entheologues: Conversations with leading Psychedelic Thinkers, Explorers and Researchers* (Kyandara Publishing, 2009)

- *Mountain Spirits: Embodying the Sacred in Mescalero Apache Tradition* (VDM Publishing, 2009)

For more information, check out Martin's weekly podcast, "The Entheogenic Evolution," available at iTunes and at www.entheogenic.podomatic.com

CPSIA information can be obtained at www.ICGtesting.com
Printed in the USA
LVOW071245250911

247780LV00002B/103/P